ONTESTED **SYMMETRIES** AND OTHER PREDICAMENTS IN ARCHITECTURE **PRESTON SCOTT COHEN**

CONTESTED SYMMETRIES AND OTHER PREDICAI

PRINCETON ARCHITECTURAL PRESS NEW YORK

NTS IN ARCHITECTURE **PRESTON SCOTT COHEN**

Published by
Princeton Architectural Press
37 East Seventh Street
New York, NY 10003

For a catalog of books published by Princeton Architectural Press,
call toll free 800.722.6657 or visit www.papress.com.

Editor: Mark Lamster
Book design: Scott Cohen and Cameron Wu
Cover design: Deb Wood
Typeset in Bembo and Syntax.

Special Thanks: Nettie Aljian, Ann Alter, Amanda Atkins, Jan
Cigliano, Jane Garvie, Mia Ihara, Clare Jacobson, Anne Nitschke,
Lottchen Shivers, Tess Taylor, and Jennifer Thompson of
Princeton Architectural Press—Kevin C. Lippert, publisher

Printed and bound in Singapore

Library of Congress Cataloging-in-Publication Data

Cohen, Preston Scott.
  Contested symmetries and other predicaments in architecture /
Preston Scott Cohen.— 1st ed.
   p. cm.
Includes bibliographical references.
ISBN 1-56898-250-X (alk. paper)
  1. Cohen, Preston Scott—Themes, motives. 2. Architecture,
  Modern—20th century—United States—Designs and plans.
  3. Geometry in architecture. 4. Symmetry 5. Projective geo-
  metry 6. Perspective 7. Architecture, Baroque—Italy I. Title.
  NA737.C63 A4 2001
  720'.92—dc21   00-011301

Foreword
Geometry and the Mediation of Architectural Conflicts:
Comments on the Work of Scott Cohen
Rafael Moneo

In the past, treatises on architecture began with a discussion of origin; as such, all aspiring architects were obliged to learn geometry. Triangles, circles, ovals, the calculation of areas, and the tracing of tangents—such were the geometrical figures that, from the early Renaissance until the nineteenth century, were used to initiate architects in the study of Euclidean geometry. Early treatises prescribed architecture based on planar construction. It was through the assembly and connection of planes that buildings were conceived. Even the most complex Gothic cathedrals can be seen as the result of the manipulation of planes and the erection of scaffolding from which surfaces, first drawn in two dimensions, arose to define walls, arches, and columns. The need for a balanced structure was answered with geometry; stability was achieved through symmetry.

The architect's geometric vocabulary was expanded during the Renaissance with the introduction of perspective drawing. Geometry assumed a new responsibility: representation. Since then, perspective has been used as a design tool and buildings have been illustrated with plans, sections and elevations. In addition, geometry became a discipline practiced as an essential instrument in the calculation of true forms. Stonecutting (stereotomy) became one of the fields in which the new means of representation would aid architects in the construction of domes, vaults, and arches. Geometry also played an important role in mechanical calculation.

In the twentieth century, geometry entered a period of decline. New techniques and a new aesthetic obscured its importance. Only in the work of a unique figure like Antonì Gaudi does geometry remain essential; Gaudi used it as a tool for construction, as an instrument to handle materials rationally both in terms of form and building techniques. Le Corbusier's use of an idealized planar geometry, where regulating lines and echoes of the golden section support the desired organization of the façade, is but a token of the fading role played by geometry as an actual tool.

Today, geometry has disappeared in a world that strives more and more to be numerical. Digitalization reaffirms the Cartesian grid while it seems to liberate form from any constraint. New techniques in modelling allow architects to proceed without the difficulty of unbalanced structures; geometry is no longer determined by the demands of construction. Thus architects can enjoy complete freedom, able to represent and build without any limits imposed by geometry. *Delenda est geometria* (geometry must be destroyed) seems to be an apt motto for today's architect.

The arbitrariness and lack of restraint that characterizes this new era of formal freedom raises questions about other paradigms that seek to rediscover the precisely determined, purposeful, or inevitable attributes of form. Preston Scott Cohen's architecture establishes such paradigms by making them the irrefutable keys to uncovering the implicit content in his projects. His work as an architect—presented here in a highly anticipated volume—takes a particularly novel turn toward the instrumentalization of projective geometry as a means by which to revel anew in the discipline of architecture. And, as a result, both architecture and geometry are transformed. Through the lens of geometry, the actualization of form is reconceived—out of place and time, apart from the nostalgic reiteration of historical architectural processes. In this transferral of reality into another set of ideas, the use of projective geometry as an instrument of architectural investigation transcends and transforms the burdensome question of type. Geometry becomes a tool for deconstructing memory. Cohen offers us geometry that again can be an extremely valuable tool for an architect, and his work offers a rare testimony to the relevance of this discipline in the development of new design methods.

The very title of this book, *Contested Symmetries*, suggests the manner in which Cohen understands the complex nature of architecture as it emerges from disciplinary conflicts. In examining two Italian villas, he uncovers the problems earlier architects faced when adapting a well-established type to very specific circumstances. In the Palazzo Gambara—"a castello transformed into a villa"—the façade Cohen analyzes is a result of an added stair from the nineteenth century. Only an attempt to give the entrance a certain form of dignity and decorum can explain the architect's intervention, which distorts and divides the main hall on the upper floor. But the stair also disrupts the garden façade and needs to be concealed. Cohen observes that the solution to this peculiar problem, "precipitated the development of extraordinarily dis-

rupted, multiplied and rigorously interlocked patterns of bilateral symmetry." Cohen assumes the difficult task of the stair's architect. He begins by explaining the original condition of the Palazzo Gambara, before the nineteenth-century intervention, revealing the misalignment of the front and rear façades. He suggests that the unknown architect sought to subtly connect the two with the help of the stair and the introduction of a serliana (in the style popularized by Andrea Palladio and Sebastiano Serlio) unrelated to the ancillary windows below it. With precise and effective diagrams, Cohen shows how and why the stair is placed off axis with the front façade. But his analysis doesn't end there. The addition of the serliana in the façade meant rearranging the windows, creating interlocked patterns of bilateral symmetry, evidence of an unconscious and acute vision. Are we to accept such a sophisticated resolution as a result of chance without any explicit awareness of the conflict? It is astonishing to see now—and we do so thanks to Cohen's analysis—as many as eight different episodes of bilateral symmetry contained in the final façade.

I should emphasize that Cohen's study of the Palazzo Gambara's rear façade is not limited to the formal aspects of the façade itself. Rather than describing the vertical façade as independent from the building's structure—an approach present, as he reminds us, in both Colin Rowe's and Peter Eisenman's studies of Venetian palazzo façades—his explanation of Palazzo Gambara's façade focuses on the stair, a structural element, that offers a solution to the salient conflict. In other words, his understanding of the architectural phenomenon implies a complex, comprehensive view, that goes beyond a simple formal analysis of the vertical plane. Manipulating the stair, the architect was able to arrive at an "extraordinary synthesis" in the rear whereby "the disposition of any single symmetrical group now necessitates and is necessitated by the disposition of all the others that together contest the heretofore totalizing system of order and symmetry." Here are the contested symmetries. The architect, with the help of a purely architectural maneuver, resolves the conflict in the façade. Architecture in this instance is born from conflicts that require resolution. Architects use symmetries to mediate in the contests that produce buildings. Cohen re-enacts conflicts and discovers the immanence of the built reality.

With the Villa Tauro, under very different conditions, Cohen makes a similar discovery, revealing an attempt to reform a well-established Venetian type to the new *terraferma* colonization. Scott Cohen reminds us that we have learned—from reading Manfredo Tafuri's books such as *Venezia e il Rinascimento* and *Ricerca del Rinascimento*—that, either consciously or unconsciously, architects in the past have made typological transformations due to social and economic conditions. And so Cohen explains to us why "in the early sixteenth century, Venetian palaces began to feature stacked *piani nobili*, a horizontal stratification that denied vertical hierarchy." He proceeds to show us that unlike the Palazzo Gambara, where we understand the rear façade based on vertical axes, in Villa Tauro we can identify "overlapping horizontal bands." Furthermore, he notes that when "exported to the countryside, the tripartite type was no longer subject to the constraints of a dense urban context." Once more, as a result of a stair intruding on a larger room—that plays the role of the Venetian *androne*—we find a façade in which symmetry "depends upon how one looks at it.…Optically contingent it flickers in and out of focus." Here, the symmetry is unstable and we perceive it in different ways depending on where we direct our gaze. We should talk of "apparent symmetry" more than of "bilateral symmetry." Again, the attempt to absorb the stairs without disturbing the façade is ultimately responsible for this uneven, unstable symmetry so carefully described by Scott Cohen.

A reading of these analyses begs the already anticipated question: "Were these earlier architects aware of all the subtleties discovered by Cohen? Or should we say that Cohen, reinventing the architectural conflicts and explaining their resolution, should today be con-

sidered the true architect of the palazzo and the villa? With his precise reading, Cohen unveils a more profound layer of reality, one that is based on a structure that belongs only to the building and shows us that buildings have their own immanence, regardless of their time, place, or architect.

With "Elliptical Congruencies," geometry transcends two-dimensional conditions and embodies— when assuming three-dimensional concerns—our own sensory experience. The case Cohen offers us is quite astonishing. Geometry, at first glance, seems to be a mere instrument for accommodating a sacristy in the corner of a rather conventional church. But this corner must simultaneously make inconspicuous certain conditions of conflict between the sacristy and its façade that appears to be predetermined. Making this assumption, Cohen clarifies a sophisticated design process involving the resolution of the intersections of cylinders and a cone with the vertical façades. The result reveals an impressive facility with the use of projective geometry. Was the architect of the sacristy of San Carlo ai Catinari acquainted with conical intersections and familiar with the field of projective geometry, which was established in the middle of the seventeenth century by the French architect and mathematician Gerard Desargues, and to which his con-temporary Blaise Pascal later made significant contributions? Evidence alludes to the presence of an unconscious and immensely acute architectural vision. Is it possible that the anonymous architect of the sacristy of San Carlo ai Catinari employed the most advanced theoretical knowledge to resolve a conflict blending both the urban conditions of the church and the interior lighting? It seems unusual that the baroque architect would apply such sophisticated geometry so discreetly without celebrating its presence.

In baroque Rome, we are used to seeing architecture with remarkably drawn geometrical intricacies, but I don't know of any other example where such a direct application of the most recent geometrical theory helped an architect resolve a rather practical problem. Thus, I am inclined to believe that Cohen, by re-enacting this hidden architectural episode, is the true architect of the sacristy. His graphic diagrams describe the problem and its solution much more clearly than any other description. The talent of the architect is shown best when, desiring a proper unity among parts, he is required to transform a cylinder into a cone. Indeed, it is compelling to watch an architect undertaking such a sophisticated application of geometry. Thanks to Cohen's analysis, I can imagine an architect who celebrated the way his disciplined study led him to solve a real architectural conflict. Scott Cohen should have enjoyed no less pleasure when, walking around San Carlo ai Catinari, he imagined the invention of this sacristy window.

In Chapter 4, "Inversive Projections: Taylorian Perspective Apparatus" Cohen revisits perspective in the light of projective geometry as a specific case of homology. Cohen's love of distorted symmetries leads him to show how Brooke Taylor's method implied an inverted and distorted symmetry before starting the procedure of projecting and sectioning. The use of the computer allows him to render the Taylorian device in an unprecedented three-dimensional way. In so doing, projective geometry reinforces the fact that it was the continuous use of perspective that trained the eyes of seventeenth century builders to see the discipline and principles inherited from the Greeks in a new and magnificent way. All the old elements of geometry could be defined for the sake of projections in a manner that was astonishingly close to our own sight. Cohen acutely presents the Taylorian two-dimensional projections relative to their implicit three-dimensional projection, the "apparatus." With the instrumental role played by the computer, this analysis isolates a complex and elusive subject—the representation of an object—in the incredible maze of planes and lines required by the Taylorian procedure. Cohen's devotion to geometry as representation and as three-dimensional transformation is clearly manifested in this astonishing collection of plates. Rather than indulge in the

production of capricious fantastic forms, the capacity of the computer becomes a new instrument of architectural inquiry. The modelled projector seen in this book would not be possible without the aid of the computer, but showing it in this way lays bare an entire process, the performance of the perspective machine itself. For Cohen, the computer allows for a reinvestment in the "eyes of geometry." We are invited to look again.

Cohen's interest in symmetry and geometry is very much present in his own work. It isn't difficult to see in some of his earliest works, such as the Siesta Key House, echoes of his research of Venetian villas. He openly confesses it when saying that the Siesta Key House "is rooted in the analysis and reformulation of several Northern Italian vernacular villas." With its deceptive central axis, the house resists any attempt to be read as symmetrical. The lessons that he learned in Palazzo Gambara have been applied carefully here. The center of the primary façade is dominated by a complex sequence in which the two main axes of the plan coalesce, one mastering the void of the living room, the other reflecting the powerful structure of the stair. One would be inclined to relate such an important episode to the entrance, and yet the entrance is displaced toward the north and, as a matter of fact, it happens to stay at a lower level. The tension established by this deceptive symmetry affects the overall house and manifests its presence both in plan and section. The consciously handled conflict between the two halves of the house results in a formal instability that resists conventional interpretation. Cohen's observations when talking about the Villa Tauro are particularly pertinent here. The system of order "makes its appearance [at the Siesta Key House] according to the vicissitudes of perception and expectations...it flickers in and out of focus."

It would be misleading to believe that these problems of symmetry (and seriality) are merely volumetrically and planimetrically oriented. Indeed, they permeate the entire Siesta Key House. He doesn't forget the structural role stairs play in Italian villas and here it can be said that the stair transcends a strict instrumentality as it reveals both the movement and the spatial order of the house. The stairs are not, as in Palazzo Gambara, celebrating the immersion of the villa in the landscape. Instead they emphasize the introverted character of the house, which aspires to create its own world, ignoring the trivial neighborhood surroundings. Cohen's capacity to maintain this variety of agendas while dealing with sophisticated geometrical mechanisms and devices for generating the architectural form is impressive. He shows an ability to maintain a high level of procedural discourse while developing an architectural program and thus prevents his architecture from falling into a limited formalism.

His latest projects—Torus House, the house in Montague, and the proposal for the Temporary MoMA—enter different territory. The studies of perspective and projective geometry have broadened his approach to design. New procedures and mechanisms allow him to geometrically manipulate form, bringing him a new architectural vocabulary. In architecture of the past, forms were conceived and constructed with the help of geometry. Today, an architect like Scott Cohen shows that the time has arrived once again to transform geometry (or geometric experiences/geometric events) into built form. We should recognize the central role played by computers in this re-emergence of geometry. The difficulty of representing curves once limited their use. Cohen shows that the ease with which curves can be drawn and manipulated has made them an extremely attractive instrument for enlarging the world of architectural form.

The Montague House reflects a design process that is an effective coalition of arbitrariness, the use and transformation of traditional patterns, and a site-condition interpretation. Arbitrariness is introduced when the so-called "terminal line"—"[a] line contained within the boundaries of a single surface"—is defined. The process begins once this surface is taken as a given. The surface plays the role of an encoded

genetic message that will make this specific and tangible work of architecture unique and different. So Cohen produces a serpentine sunken line that completely transforms the surface. He then transforms the surface into a prism—by simply folding it up—and maintains the embedded terminal line, which looks like a scar. Afterward, he projects from this prism a second, distorted prism. The first prism will hold the rather conventional house program; the second one will hold a carport and a landscaped terrace. All of this can be understood as an arbitrary procedure. But, going further, one can see how known types are transformed. One discerns the importance of the rather conventional roads that cut the surfaces and prevent a single-minded reading. Arbitrariness is a starting point that can be adjusted to specific conditions. The inevitable arbitrariness that seems to be in every architectural beginning is tamed by reality; even recognizing the importance of arbitrariness, the architect manifests his ability to react with freedom.

Though some similarities can be seen between the Montague House and the earlier House on Longboat Key, it is important to note the differences. Cohen has left behind the conventional "cardboard" abstraction of the House on Longboat Key and now claims that the surface continuity his work is demanding can be achieved with wood structural ribs and wood-concrete panel cladding. The tectonic expression that architecture enjoyed for centuries disappears thanks to an artificially generated, infinitely complex form. Geometry is no longer the vehicle that enables construction. Geometry prevails. It doesn't help construction, instead it imposes the built form. There is nothing wrong with that. I find it natural that a machine like the computer brings geometry to unknown—or unseen—worlds. And therefore, as a consequence, architects long to introduce these new forms to construction. Without developing a new language, architects enjoy this "new geometrical landscape" so easily generated by the computer and so effectively providing new ways of relating with the existing topography. Among these architects, the geometrically rigorous work of Preston Scott Cohen is one of the most serious attempts to break new ground.

The Torus House advances a no less ambitious program. The terminal line, tying together the planes of the roof and floor with a perforated void, winds around a stair that allows people to walk up directly from the parking area to the roof. The two planes, activated by the "terminal line," merge with both landscapes. A ramped foyer calls to mind Le Corbusier; Cohen always pays attention to a building's entrances and certain echoes of the Le Corbusian promenade (an almost mandatory memory!) resound in his work. Even when using new methods, Cohen does not ignore architectural history. The Torus House brings us a contemporary version of the Le Corbusian procedure of overlapping horizontal planes, with the landscape serving as background. And yet these horizontal planes express the present desire for instability, as reflected in the waving and undulating surfaces transformed by the terminal line. The house can also be seen as "a compressed tower, its top and bottom flared into undulating horizontal surfaces." Once more, Cohen escapes from pure formalism by including other interests. That allows him to master his work without becoming a slave of his own procedural devices. This reading of the Torus House, instead of being a distraction, becomes an asset that gives it a sense of actuality. In my view, this is where its interest resides.

A debt to modern architecture is openly recognized by Cohen in his project for the Temporary MoMA, which references the work of Le Corbusier and Mies van der Rohe. After crafting the corner entrance, he brings the pre-existing grid into play, as a token of neutrality and flexibility, and centers his interest in the ceiling. It is in the ceiling where the architect's freedom is manifested: the hierarchic and static condition of the Miesian grid is denied by an agitated ceiling where, once more, the geometries afforded by the computer prevail. Meanwhile, the undulating drapery of the wall alludes with its movement, to the restless condition of contemporary art.

What seems to me particularly admirable in Scott Cohen's latest work is that, in spite of introducing a high level of arbitrariness by means of projection and the "terminal line," he effectively maintains his external agenda. He always has been able to give his work the character he wanted it to have. The Torus House— and the same can be said about the Montague House and the Temporary MoMA project—has been mastered by the architect. They are what he wanted them to be. His process is extremely sophisticated and yet it does not usurp his authority. Cohen's architecture is not an example of mechanical determinism—it is the architect's wishes and sensitivity that prevail. This is not a minor achievement; geometry is once again a great tool in the hands of the architect.

Introduction
Predicaments and Surrogates

This book examines how predicaments generate architecture. Buildings fall prey to predicaments when architects, in attempting to overcome seemingly insurmountable obstacles and to conceal all that must be done in order to do so, resort to the use of strange and exceptional forms. The process of unearthing and introducing architectural predicaments can expose and ultimately lead to the revision of norms, assumptions and standards that usually remain undetected in architecture.

The study of architectural predicaments is not aimed at the production of new and conspicuous forms, although this book certainly contains its share of these. It deals instead with the examination of the boundary between the straightforward and the deceptive, the conventional and the decadent. The buildings to be addressed in the first section of this book (the Palazzo Gambara, the Villa Tauro, the Sacristy of San Carlo ai Catinari), therefore, initially appear unexceptional. They share scale, language, and material with their neighbors and can be immediately identified with a series. Yet within these structures, there are episodes of internal complexity camouflaged in normative pattern—architecture behaving as it ought not to. These episodes are anomalous primarily because they deviate from a readily accepted architectural norm. And this immediately raises questions about the status of norms themselves—their relative stability, their persistence, and how and to whom they are legible.

Architecture has motives and aspirations independent of the raw forces that shape everyday material culture—it is, and should be, a site of surplus and strangeness. It is capable of eliciting intellectual pleasure, whether or not it is obedient to the pleasure principles of the market. But the excessiveness of architecture stimulates the most intellectual pleasure when it comes about by some kind of necessity, rather than by authorial will or expression. And even though successive waves of modernization have apparently swept away architecture's capacity to generate quandaries, it is, nevertheless, still compelling to seek the rules and scenarios that make strangeness mandatory—producing, instead of an easy decorative program, an architecture full of tension and struggle.

Yet architects today largely reject difficulty, avoiding this sort of motivated complexity. Flush with the excitement of the latest technological advancements or material fetishes, and seduced by the boundless possibilities of the present, they pursue an architecture that might best be described as postproblematic—an architecture in which few forms are considered either unacceptable or unreachable. The post-problematic condition has allowed some architects to explore a new range of unconstrained forms. For others, it has seemingly provided a reprieve from the shackles of form-making altogether. Indeed, architecture has become a discipline of disinterestedness, arbitrariness, and easily digestible decoration.

The development of the flatfish (*heterosomata*) provides a good illustration of the kind of motivated strangeness architects today so rarely confront in their work. Like most fish, the flatfish begins by swimming with the axis of its body perpendicular to the ocean floor, one eye on either side of its symmetrical face. But as this fish matures, its feeding habits require it to swim close to the bottom of the ocean. So the flatfish adapts. As it swims progressively closer to the ocean floor, its body gradually rotates to a position parallel to the floor surface, while the eye that would otherwise face the dark ocean surface slowly migrates to the "top" side of its body. A mature flatfish, then, swims parallel to the ocean floor, both eyes on one side of its face. And for those of us who expect symmetry in our fish, this is somewhat disturbing.

Nowadays, architecture can hardly be compared to the flatfish. The flatfish distorts because it must; and although it does so regularly and for practical and involuntary reasons, some of us continue to find it strange. Architecture too needs to be strange and to keep being strange in order not to die off. Yet architecture rarely exhibits this sort of recognizable and purposeful distortion. An architecture that is compelled to distort, and that ultimately highlights and questions norms, requires the invention of surrogate problems.

If architecture is incapable of regularly distorting like the flatfish, it can be impelled to do so by the posing of insoluble problems. Architects could create problems, vigorously attempt to solve them, and never be able to. Architecture would thus keep itself alive by remaining an unfulfilled promise. The dilemma, of course, is that the very idea of an unfulfilled promise is widely presumed to be outmoded and suspect; it implies some sort of formal ideal that can never be attained. In the post-problematic era, the idea of

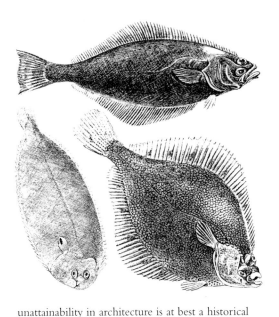

0.1 Fish of the pleuronectiformes order. Right-eyed flounders and soles.

13

unattainability in architecture is at best a historical project; today's proprieties are too diffuse, vast, and inexact to support legible formal tension. There is little in terms of form to keep the architect's intentions from being disposed immediately, completely, and without problem. The few constricting norms we face today, based on building industry standards, for example, are so agonizingly restrictive that architects must either comply blindly with them, or supplant them with altogether rarified methods. The latter case creates a binary relationship between norm and exception, one that does not allow for subtlety and slyness.

But it was not always this way. The intricate and demanding language of classical architecture, for example, once provided an exacting set of limitations. Codes of decorum and order led architects into predicaments whenever strict linguistic demands conflicted with technological innovations (for example, the nineteenth and twentieth century development of structural steel and the elevator), or with specific sites, cultures, or institutional programs. In each of these situations, grammatical problems inevitably arose if architects attempted to perfect or correctly apply the classical language while simultaneously responding to a range of unrelated and at times contradictory demands.

What is interesting about the Palazzo Gambara,

0.2

0.3

0.4

14

0.2, 0.3, 0.4
Advanced by Gerard Desargues during the first half of the seventeenth century, projective geometry focuses on the invariant geometrical properties (magnitudes) shared by all sections of one or more projections of the same object. That is, it seeks to define invariants under transformations referred to as "projection" and/or "section." In this system, conic sections are perspectives of one another or of a circle. The apex of a cone can be identified as the eyepoint of a perspective. See: Morris Kline, "Projective Geometry," *Scientific American*, January 1965.

the Villa Tauro, and the Sacristy of San Carlo ai Catinari is not that their architects were exceptional, or that they aimed to perfect the classical language. Probably, neither was the case. What is intriguing is that these architects were forced to grapple with the limits of an architectural language that they inherited. In both cases, however, something prevented them from complying with the rules and regulations of that language. Utility and decorum were not altogether reconciled. There are moments when the architects, struggling vainly to balance pragmatic demands with the imperatives of classical grammar, lose control. Their very inability to tackle the problems that confronted them reveals something of the struggle in which they were embroiled. The intent of this book is to demonstrate that such errors can be used today as evidence of a mode of thought. A virtuoso architect would have dispelled these problems and the results would not require explanation here.

In the Palazzo Gambara, disruptions of symmetry are caused by functional and economic factors that play out over time. These distortions have little to do with the desire to create or enter into an artistic play. Villa Tauro and the Sacristy of San Carlo ai Catinari, on the other hand, appear to be willed problems. Unlike Gambara, which seems to have unwittingly trapped its

architects and builders in a series of architectural contingencies, the architects of the other two projects—also unknown—clearly volunteered for the job.

The sacristy is particularly compelling because it joins architecturally contested symmetries with projective geometric procedures. This represents an extraordinary departure from traditional architectural practice: evidence of the concealment of conflicts is corroborated by another discipline, projective geometry (figs 0.2-0.4). At the sacristy, congruency among conic and cylindrical sections allows unusual elements to disappear into conventional architectural symmetries. The effect of concealment can be compared to the projective technique of anamorphosis, a procedure usually used in painting. An extreme case of conventional perspective, anamorphosis produces distorted images that can only be seen undistorted from a peculiar position or by using a special instrument. Palazzo Gambara, Villa Tauro, and the Sacristy of San Carlo ai Catinari obscure various disturbances through simultaneous, intertwined symmetries—anamorphoses executed within the language of architecture. They become accessible through the instruments of analysis presented in this book.

The case of projection that most aptly compares to the flatfish, however, is the perspective method developed in England during the early eighteenth century by Brook Taylor. Close examination of his system uncovers a distortion of symmetry that is a felicitous and entirely practical consequence of a projective function. Projection flattens objects by transferring three-dimensional properties onto a two-dimensional plane—the drawing surface. This book presents a computer model of Taylor's device showing that behind his two-dimensional perspective lies a three-dimensional projective process that rotates and inverts the object being projected. Two symmetrically opposite projections result, orthographic and perspectival, each a distortion of the other. Thus, projection is shown to produce an episode of regularly-occurring distortion. This contrasts with such episodes in architecture that usually do not become instrumental or regularized. The most extraordinary distortions in architecture remain singular anomalies, the scattered byproducts of a discipline fraught with irregularity. Like obsolete processes of adaptation, such anomalies lie dormant until rekindled by delayed incidents of curiosity.

By the end of the twentieth century, it seemed anachronistic to generate subtly camouflaged episodes, such as those illustrated in the first chapters of this book. With classicism's persistent imperative for coherence and symmetry superceded by the less circumscribed palette of modernism, distortion would have to be generated without the imperative to conceal violations or errors. With nothing to hide, only the devices of deception remained and the game of camouflage seemed all but impossible to play. The Torus House introduces a problem with geometrical consequences that, unlike the sacristy and Villa Tauro, *expose* internal contadictions. To what extent can a house continue to evoke the form of a torus after it has been subjected to all the practical conditions necessary to be a normally functioning house? A torus has neither top nor bottom, and must exist *en plein air*—conditions that are essentially incompatible with a domestic program.

The struggle to preserve the idea of the torus, then, produces a rather peculiar house. Of course, there is no reason why a house must evoke the idea of the torus. But without it, there would be no problem at all. Fortuitously, in the case of the Temporary MoMA project, the institution contributed to the formation of the architectural problem. The program demands a central lobby space on one edge of a windowless warehouse. So positioned, the lobby would be denied an exterior view, and would also be denied the bustling activity that might come about were the lobby positioned in the building's center. The problem, then, is to make palatable the idea that the lobby is embedded somewhere deep within the building, even though it is on the edge. Thus, predictable sequences of movement and the normative columnar structure succumb to transformation.

This book outlines a mode of architectural thought that looks for the problems inherent in apparently stable structures; a mode of thought that creates architectural problems where there are none, and strives not to make something that looks radically strange and different, but to elaborate upon the contest between norm and anomaly. Yet these predicaments are surrogate problems; they stand in for those that architecture once initiated without authorial will.

1
Contested Symmetries: Palazzo Gambara

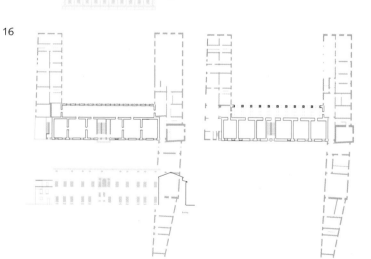

1.1 Palazzo Gambara, Veralanuova, Brescia. These plans show the 18th and 19th century interventions and additions in green. In Brescia, beginning during the 15th century, loggias were occasionally added to castelli of this type.

1.2 Palazzo Gambara. Loggia entrance.

Located in what was part of the Veneto *terraferma* until the dissolution of the Venetian state in 1797, the Palazzo Gambara evolved from a feudal stronghold into a villa.[1] The main stair was inserted in the mid-nineteenth century, almost four hundred years after the building of the original *castello* out of which the palace evolved. It is located nearly in the center of the palazzo, directly behind the front loggia, dividing in two what had been the great hall of the palace (figs. 1.1 & 1.2). Yet this type of stair, a switchback, cannot comply with symmetry given that the stair's center—the gap between opposite runs—is not an axis that can be occupied. Moreover, since the loggia is composed of ten bays, a symmetrical location for the staircase entrance was precluded in advance. But these were not the only impediments to symmetry. The stair was placed perpendicular to the longitudinal axis of the room, leaving insufficient space for an interior landing at the loggia entry. Therefore, the entrance was required to open directly onto one run of the switchback and could not align with the center of the entire stairwell. In addition, the pre-existing context included a loggia situated in such a way that none of the axes of its bays quite align with the axes of rooms behind. Under these circumstances, the stair becomes a unique element because it carries the misalignment of the

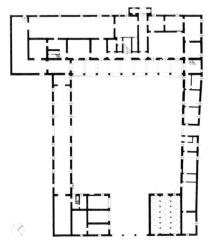

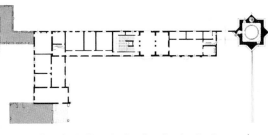

1.4 Corte Castiglioni, Marcaria, Casatico. Construction in several stages from the 15th to the 17th century.

1.3 Villa Soncini, Brescia, 17th century. Stair hall added during the 18th century, when ideal axes became imperative.

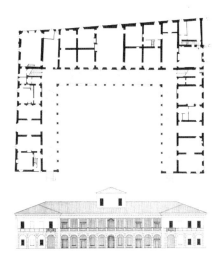

17

front through to the back façade where windows affixed to the stair disrupt the window pattern associated with the rooms. The result is an extraordinary series of interconnected symmetries.

It is puzzling that the most important and commodious room was forsaken for a stair that further enriched and gave visible expression to problems of order inherent to the main wing of the palazzo. Other Brescian villas with plans similar to Gambara's do not exhibit such contradictions. Many are more rigidly ordered, while others include idiosyncracies that do not give rise to rigorously combined patterns of order (like Villa Soncini, fig. 1.3). Usually, the stair provides a grand entry sequence by either fully occupying a room and running laterally within it (as in Corte Castiglioni and Villa Menafoglio, figs. 1.4 & 1.5), or by being laterally disposed within a room extending from, and as deep as, the loggia (as in the Lechi villas in Erbusco and Montirone, figs. 1.6 & 1.7). In some cases the plan is deep enough to accommodate a significant place of arrival following the stair (as in Villa Soncini), or a place of introduction—a prelude to the stair (as in Villa Fulcis, fig. 1.8-overleaf). The U-shaped peristyles of the forecourts at the villas Lechi, to name just two such examples, are more readily associated with the *cortile* of Roman palaces than with Venetian

1.5 Villa Menafoglio, Verese, 1755. Perhaps the first U-shaped plan in the Verese area oriented toward a private garden with emphasis on central axis.

1.6 Villa Lechi at Erbusco, Eastern Brescia, 16th and 17th century. An early example of a villa with an open courtyard, a type that only became common during the 18th century.

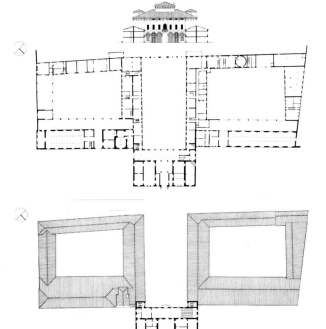

1.7 Villa Lechi at Montirone, Brescia, 1739-60. Antonio Turbino (1676-1756) architect.

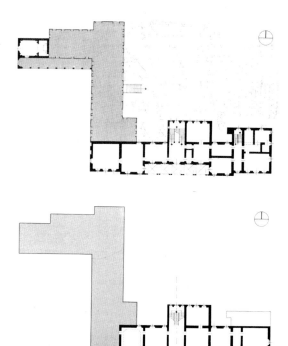

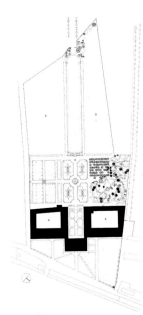

1.9 Villa Lechi at Montirone, Brescia.

1.8 Villa Fulcis, Belluno, early 17th c. The central room was enlarged in the 19th century and the stair was added. It replaced a narrower stair that had flanked the entrance hall.

precedents. In both of these exemplary villas, as in a typical Roman palace, the stair is located near the corner of the *cortile*. The main loggia of Palazzo Gambara, if considered to be a fragment of a *cortile* from a Roman model, implies that what is currently the palazzo's secondary, or rear façade, should be the front, as in the Villa Lechi at Montirone (fig. 1.9). The plan of Gambara, by referring the rear to a condition of frontality, lends added significance to the added serliana and its effect on the composition of other windows on the rear façade.

To put it simply, the stair in Gambara denies the decorous implication of its approximately central position. The contradictory impulses that it displays may be attributed to the architect's incompetence or to the patron's desire to emulate continental classical models under restrictive conditions that stymied such developments. But such alibis cannot account for the specific type and peculiar disposition of stairs that refer to those found in Venetian palaces after the late fifteenth century, where, within the tripartite plan, a central hall (the *portego*) is flanked by two rows of smaller rooms, one of which contains a modest switchback stair (fig. 1.10). Illuminated by two small windows at mid-landing, these stairs are constricted, steep, and uncommodious. In Gambara, the stairs are similarly

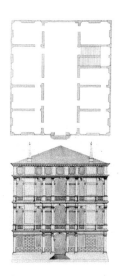

1.10 Palazzo Giustiniani a San Vidal, Venice.

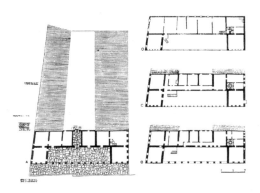

1.11 Fondaco dei Turchi, Venice. The ten bay loggia was flanked by stout corner towers.

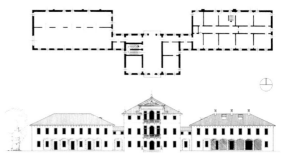

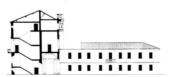

1.13 Palazzo Gambara. Section showing the 19th century stair.

1.14 Villa Vescovile, Belluno, 1711-13. Paolo Tremignon, architect. Service wings flank the relatively small main body.

1.12 Palazzo Giustiniani II, Venice.

located in a row of rooms. As in Venice, the rooms are reached from a common hall and passage between them is interrupted by the stair. Thus, Gambara is half a Venetian palazzo turned ninety degrees to the original axis of approach from the Grand Canal.

Though similar to the internal stair of the Venetian palazzo, the stair in Gambara sets up a sequence from the exterior that recalls an earlier Venetian precedent, the *casa-fondaco*.[2] Palazzo Gambara superficially resembles this type to the extent that its loggia is the lower level in a broad two story façade and is not one segment of a peristile or the side of a *cortile*. Transported from Constantinople, and taking its earliest form in the Fondaco dei Turchi (Turkish Warehouse) of the twelfth century, the *casa-fondaco* functioned within the Venetian mercantile economy and served as the seat of a family's wealth and power (fig. 1.11). The lower level was dedicated to commerce, and the upper to domestic life. Upper and lower plans were composed identically, however, and maintained a distinctive tripartite configuration: a central hall, defining an axis through from front to back, was flanked by two side bays of smaller rooms. The front loggia, the *androne*, and side rooms served a waterside entry for loading and unloading goods, conducting business, and warehousing merchandise.

The defining sequential feature of the medieval type (and also of the Gothic palazzo) was an exterior stair located in a rear *cortile* (fig. 1.12). Hence, visitors arriving at the waterside entry would proceed through the *androne* (in which business was conducted and armor was usually displayed) to the *cortile* and then ascend the external stair to the piano nobile, while those entering from the land could immediately bypass the commercial activities, and enter directly into the domestic space. Similarly, the stair of Gambara ascends directly from the loggia to the piano nobile, as if to bypass a more functional *pian-terreno* (fig. 1.13). Unlike other Brescian villas, there is no internal connection between the stair and other rooms on the ground level. Thus, there is no internal connection between rooms on the upper and ground levels. This bifurcation of function within the same building treats the lower rooms as if they are in a *barchesse* or warehouse. Again, Gambara is inconsistent with its neighbors. In Brescian villas, the *barchesse* and other farm functioning structures were not usually embedded within the main residence (fig. 1.14). Even in the most urbane Palladian villas of the *terraferma*, the *barchesse* was attached to the main house at the sides. In other words, in the Palladian type, functional division occurred in plan, not in section.

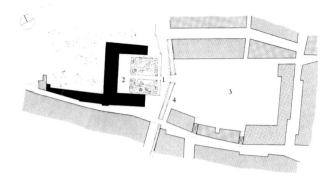

1.15 Palazzo Gambara, Veralanuova, Brescia. The moat may have once been linked to the original castello before becoming part of the garden in the 18th century.

Clearly, the sectional division of Gambara does not refer to Venice after the mid-fifteenth century, when the dual function of the *fondaco* gave way to the domestic program of the Gothic and early Renaissance palace. While remaining tripartite, the palace became narrower, deeper and taller due to the increased density of the city and the value of land. Yet, the Gambara stair does refer to the internalization of the Venetian stair, a development that was crucial to the maturation of the palace type. Primarily a functional conduit that expedited vertical communication and movement between stacked horizontal units, the Venetian palatial stair compares to a strictly utilitarian modern stair. Consuming as little premium living space as possible, it gave tangible form to Alberti's dictum that "the fewer the staircases that are in a house, the better."[3] The stair was an element of necessity that needed to be absorbed without disrupting the ideal order of the plan of rooms. This was a view that prevailed in Italy, for the most part, through the beginning of the seventeenth century.[4]

In his early-seventeenth-century treatise, *Dell' Idea della Architettura Universale*, Vincenzo Scamozzi likened the circulation in a building to the veins and arteries of the human body: invisible, regulatory, and transitory.[5] Accordingly, stairs were imbued with corporeal qualities, channeling and regulating movement within an organically integrated whole. While it could be argued that most Renaissance stairs follow Scamozzi's model, those of the Venetian palazzo serve as a particularly apt illustration. For the particular narrowness and steepness of the Venetian stair, with its small windows at landings providing only minimal illumination to indicate the prescribed course, directed and transported the body as if in the circulation system of a larger body. Movement was confined and one's view limited. Passage was not visually intelligible all at once nor was it expressed through grandeur or procession. The stair as such was not visual, either in form or in the way it conducted movement.

What is most strikingly peculiar about the Gambara stair is that it refers to the Venetian palatial antecedent even though it occupies an almost central position in the plan and is perpendicular to the axis of entry. In Venice the connection between the symbolic interior of the palace and the symbolic façades lining the primary arterial center of the city—the Grand Canal—exists mainly in two utilitarian parts, the *androne* and the staircase. In contrast, Gambara extends the entry sequence into a visual procession in depth along an axis. Thus, the Gambara stair is constricted, as it were, but only by implication and as a consequence of the expectation that it be more expansive. Though on the inside it is, like the Venetian stair, not decorous, it is nonetheless in position to dilate rather than contract a view.

The anatomical metaphor, as well as the visual connections and axial foci were in fact characteristic of the baroque, as was the U-shaped configuration of the villa. Yet, within the baroque tradition, centralized stairs were visually displayed through robust plasticity and explicit axiality. The stair at Gambara lacks this external expression. Yet, one of the two small windows on the landing, which in Venice only responded to a functional requirement, coincides with a significant axis overtly expressed immediately above the two landing windows by the serliana at the culmination of the entry sequence (see fig. 1.1). In Venice, such landing windows are all but hidden on the exterior, facing a side alley or service canal. They are unmistakably distinguished from windows on the front façade (which may include a serliana). In Gambara, however, since these small windows fall in the same plane as the serliana, it appears that what was once front and side in the Venetian precedent have been collapsed onto the rear façade of the Veralonuova Palazzo. Such an adjacency not only collides decorum with function, but implies a superimposition of two strands of the baroque, ultimately producing a third. The form of the stair invokes the baroque of immersion, the hidden and the deeply embedded from which one gains only partial glimpses and never a total comprehensive view.

Alternatively, the position and orientation of the stair evoke the baroque of extended visual connections implied by fixed positions in space running along extensive axes.

Finally, the implied rotation and collapse of the Venetian referent gives rise to an extraordinary synthesis at the rear. The disturbance caused by the stair produces linked symmetrical window groupings that call to mind the restless figures of a baroque painting, unitary in form yet vigorously interlocked or interdependent. The disposition of any single symmetrical group now necessitates and is necessitated by the disposition of all others that together contest the heretofore totalizing systems of order and symmetry. Thus the particular conditions of the unit are dependent on a whole that is only made discernable by the accumulation of incommensurable episodes.

Palazzo Gambara: Chronology

As the character of the extant feudal tower suggests, the earliest plans for the *castello* that became the Palazzo Gambara date from the mid-quattrocentro, the period during which the Gambara ascended to power as feudal lords in Pralboino and Verola Alghisia (to become Verolanuova), and in which Brescia, heretofore part of, and later to return to, the province of Lombardia, became part of the Republic of Venice.[6] The original tower stands at the intersection of the three wings of the main body of the *castello*, a configuration that was originally T-shaped (fig. 1.15). In the eighteenth century, another wing, specified in the original plans but not previously realized, was added to the northwest corner of the complex, thus completing the U-shaped portion of the present configuration. The vestiges of a moat (which divides the palazzo from the adjacent piazza), and the tower (which perhaps at one time dermarcated the centrally controlled entry to the compound, perpendicular to the current entry) is typical of a fifteenth-century, fortified, inward-looking, feudal *castello* (fig. 1.2). As the *castello* transformed into a villa, it became more extroverted, a process culminating in the nineteenth century with the completion of the loggia and forecourt facing the town square and, at the conclusion of the entry sequence, the addition of a serliana on the back façade extending views into the landscape from an added stair. Such an open (nondefensive) disposition was perhaps a late inheritance from Venice, where, because the lagoon provided fortification, the palazzo could evolve without attention to its defense.[7]

Notes

1. Carlo Perogalli and Maria Grazia Sandri, *Ville Delle Province di Bergamo e Brescia* (Milan: Edizioni Sisar, 1969), 91.

2. For an account of the Palazzo-Fontego, see Ennio Concina, *A History of Venetian Architecture*, Judith Landry, trans. (New York: Cambridge University Press, 1998), 69–113.

3. This quote is referred to by Philip L. Sohm, "The State and Domestic Staircase in Venetian Society and Politics of the Renaissance," in *L'Escalier Dans L'Architecture de la Renaissance* (Paris: Picard, 1985), 123–32. He cites L. B. Alberti, *The Ten Books on Architecture*, J. Leoni, trans. (London, 1726), I, XIII, 19; Hans-Karl Lucke, Leon Battista Alberti, *De re aedificatoria* (1485; Munich: Index Verborum, 1975), 4:19a.

4. For a general discussion of the role of stairs in renaissance palaces, see Nikolaus Pevsner, *An Outline of European Architecture* (New York: Penguin, 1943), 275–86.

5. Sohm, "The State," n. 15, 124. The source is Vincenzo Scamozzi, *Dell' Idea della Architettura Universale* (Venice: 1615), 1:312.

6. Carlo Perogalli and Maria Grazia Sandri, *Ville Delle Province di Bergamo e Brescia*, 91.

7. For an account of the effect of the lagoon on the origins of the Venetian palace, see Richard J. Goy, *Venetian Vernacular Architecture: Traditional Housing in the Venetian Lagoon* (New York: Cambridge University Press, 1989), 126.

21

1.16 Palazzo Gambara. Rear garden façade.

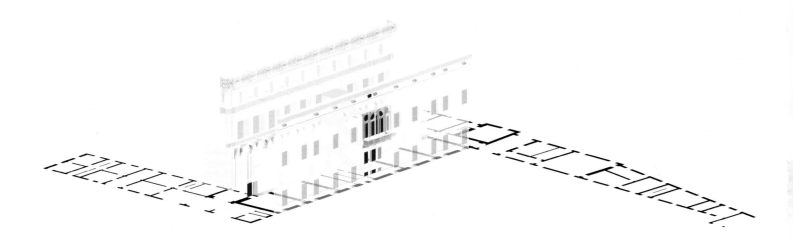

Diagrams

What is most remarkable about Palazzo Gambara is the way circumstances of the earlier *castello* combined with the arrangement of rooms and loggia bays of the palace became inextricably bound to disturbances created by a staircase added much later. The seemingly casual disruptions of the primarily serial window pattern on the rear façade might at first be considered the work of an amateur architect or the result of unforeseen modifications made to the building over time. Indeed, examples of such conditions are abundant in the region (figs. 1.18 & 1.19). Yet, if examined closely, the Gambara rear façade displays extraordinarily disrupted, multiplied, and rigorously interlocked patterns of bilateral symmetry that are too compelling for a decipherer of façades to dismiss.

The following narrative offers an explanation—albeit entirely fictional—that provides a technique for unravelling the interconnected symmetries of the palace. It implies that there are conceivable arrangements that have a certain clairvoyance about the built reality following from them. This hypothetical sequence of developments relies on a reevaluation of the cause and effect equation that generated the building. Rather than following the historical chronology, it disassembles and reassembles key episodes in order to explain the connections between the symmetries.

The story begins with an idealized pattern of rooms and loggia bays that is inherently contradictory due to the number, position, and dimension of its parts (diagram 1). The introduction of the stair exacerbates the conflicts inherent in the initial scheme (diagram 2). The surrounding context is described as an additional disturbance rather than a pre-existing constraint (diagram 4). Finally, the irregularities instantiated at the periphery by the context become systematically related to the logical contradictions in the initial pattern and stair at the heart of the palace (diagrams 5–12). Centripetal and centrifugal forces join to constitute a remarkably coherent rear façade, the new-found frontality of which is substantiated by references to Venetian antecedents and their urban context.

1.17 Palazzo Gambara. Stair and serliana intervention

1.18

1.19

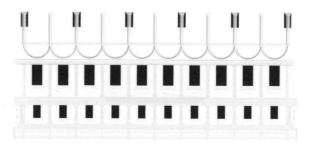

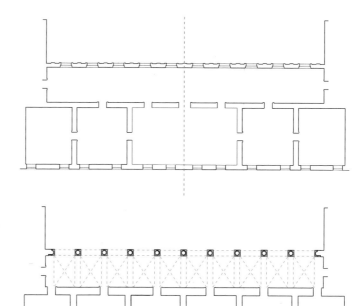

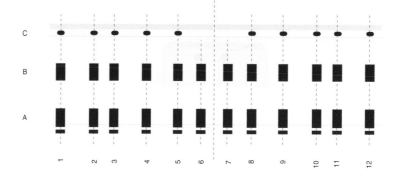

24

Diagram 1

In this schematic idealization of Palazzo Gambara, alignment of the central axis of the great hall and the loggia impedes the development of a central passage from the front to the back of the building. The dimensions of the six rooms and the loggia's ten bays on the ground floor precludes complete alignment of the constituent elements of the two series. If the doors are maintained in this way relative to one another, they fall behind columns and deny a structural correspondence between the columns and the back of the loggia. Thus, this configuration, though ideal with reference to a single central axis, is necessarily divisive and anticipates discord with the stair to come.

1

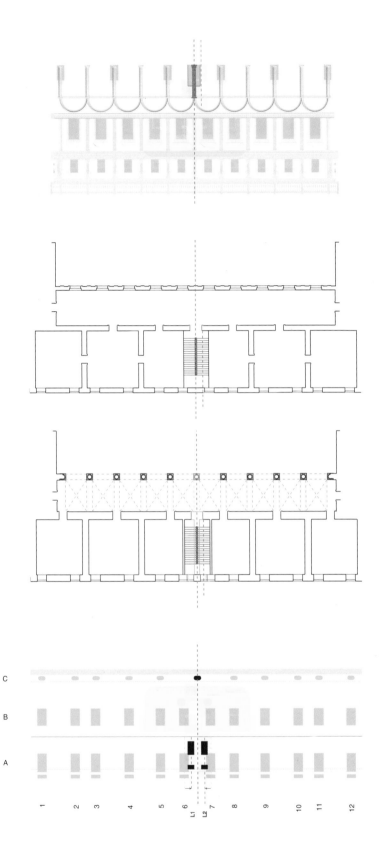

Diagram 2

Switchback staircases preclude symmetrical sequences because their central axis is a divider. In Palazzo Gambara, given the distance it is required to ascend, the stair's length leaves insufficient space for a landing behind the centrally located entrance.

C

B

A

1   2   3   4   5   6 L1 L2 7   8   9   10   11   12

2

Diagram 3
In order for the whole stair to maintain a central position, the entrance to the stairwell and one bay of the loggia are displaced such that they are centered on the first run of the switchback. This centralization requires the relocation of both the entire symmetrical group of doors and all ten bays of the loggia. Asserting the new center is a *serliana*, which appears on the rear façade at the culmination of the stair.

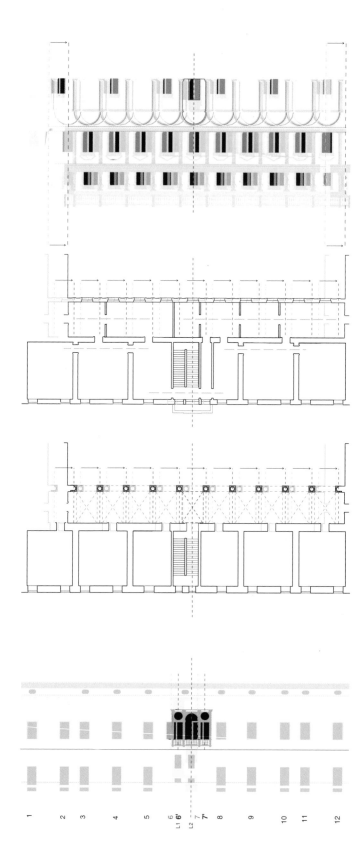

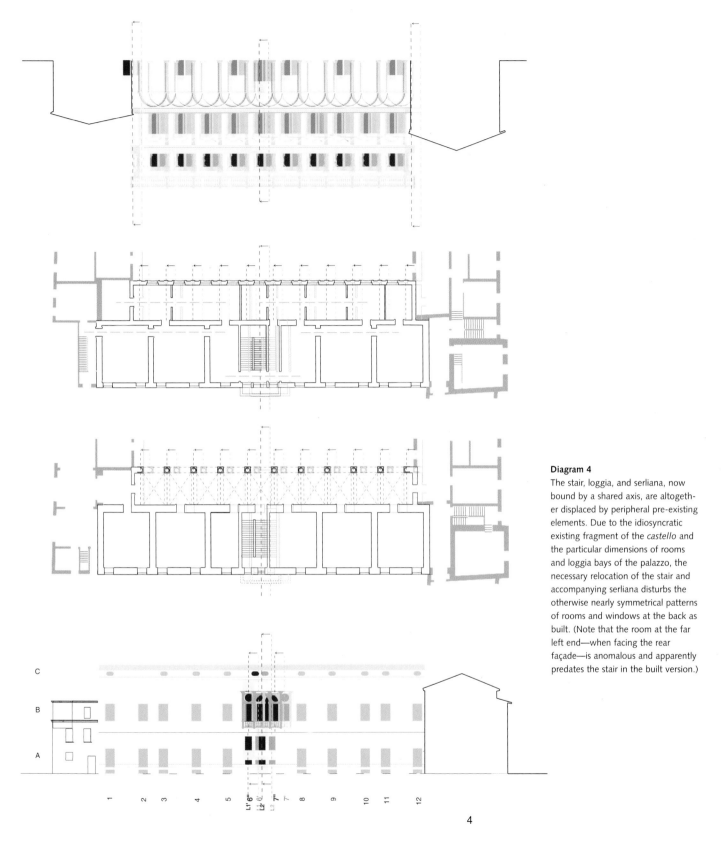

Diagram 4

The stair, loggia, and serliana, now bound by a shared axis, are altogether displaced by peripheral pre-existing elements. Due to the idiosyncratic existing fragment of the *castello* and the particular dimensions of rooms and loggia bays of the palazzo, the necessary relocation of the stair and accompanying serliana disturbs the otherwise nearly symmetrical patterns of rooms and windows at the back as built. (Note that the room at the far left end—when facing the rear façade—is anomalous and apparently predates the stair in the built version.)

4

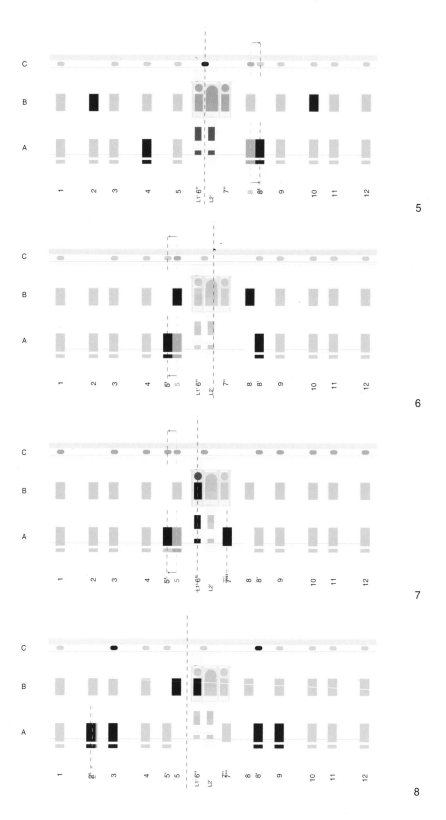

28

Diagrams 5–12: The Garden Façade
The windows on the rear façade regroup in order to integrate and compete for primacy with the anomalous windows of the serliana and stair landing.

5. Window *8A* shifts and creates a symmetrical pattern that includes the stair landing windows.

6. *5A* shifts to absorb the otherwise exceptional *8'A* into a pyramidal symmetrical pattern.

7. *5'A* simultaneously produces a pattern that claims *6"B* and *L1'A*, the left windows of the serliana and the stair landing, respectively.

8. *2A* shifts to produce a pattern which again includes the left window of the serliana.

9. *1A* shifts toward *2A* and creates a peripheral symmetrical group.

10–12. The left end of the façade including *1A*, *1B*, and *1C* shifts inward to create a series of patterns working back toward the center. Thus, centripetal disturbances associated with the external context, particularly at the left margin of the garden façade, become intricately tied to the internalized stair. Diagram 12 shows a pattern that includes characters from all other symmetries and encircles the serliana as if to contest its controlling authority.

5

6

7

8

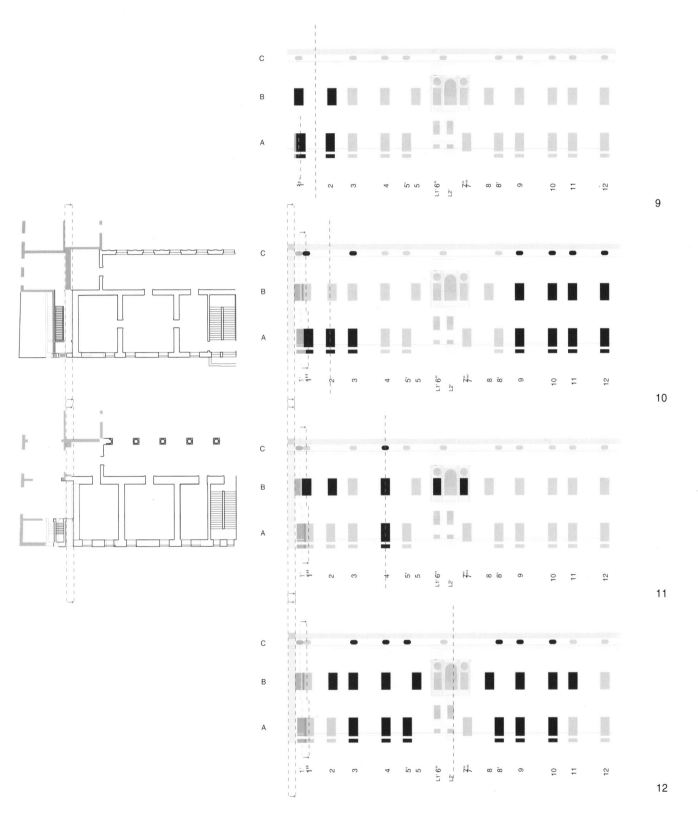

2
Regular Anomalies: Villa Tauro

2.1 Villa Tauro, Cesio Maggiore, Centenere, mid-17th century. The tripartite window series with pediment is typical of minor villas in the Feltre region.

Villa Tauro, built in the middle of the seventeenth century in Belluno, appears to be a modest descendant of the Venetian palace (fig. 2.1) The villa is based on a three bay, four wall construction system, a type that was well suited to building on the marshland of the Veneto, where it allowed standardization and minimization of horizontal structural loads. Though such a configuration placed severe limitations on light, particularly within the central hall, which could only be narrowly illuminated at its front and back ends, it was nevertheless almost uniformly adopted within the lagoon and would endure for almost four hundred years, until the palaces of Michele Sanmicheli and Jacopo Sansovino in the early- and mid-sixteenth century.[1]

Once displaced to dry ground, however, this type was bound to incur change. Nevertheless, even in Belluno, there are several examples that strictly adhere to the Venetian plan. Villa Rudio, for example, is like an urban palace taken out of its context and exposed untransformed (fig. 2.2). There are other cases, however, in which the desire to maintain the Venetian typology was evidently balanced by the need to adapt it to different conditions. Exported to the countryside, the tripartite type was no longer subject to the constraints of a dense urban context. Thus, a shallower plan (with side bays only two rooms deep) was frequently adopted

2.2 Villa Rudio, Sedico, Landris.
Completed 1685

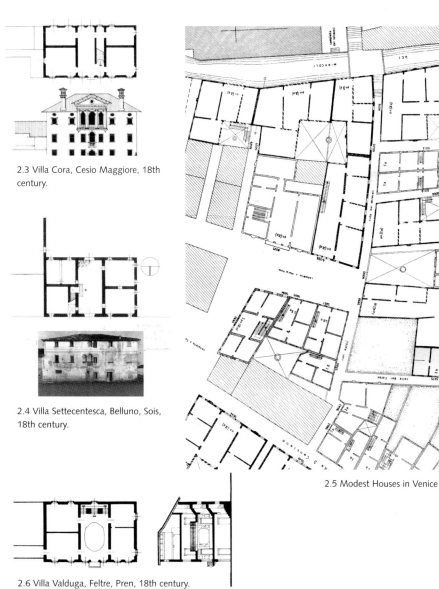

2.3 Villa Cora, Cesio Maggiore, 18th
century.

2.4 Villa Settecentesca, Belluno, Sois,
18th century.

2.5 Modest Houses in Venice

because it provided much needed light to the central hall, and the building could grow in a linear fashion along its lateral axis. In villas similar to the size of Tauro, stairs often run alongside a central hall, within it—as in Villa Cora—or immediately adjacent to it in a side bay—as in Villa Settecentesca (figs. 2.3 & 2.4). These arrangements recall modest houses and palazzetti in Venice that are far less noble than Tauro (fig. 2.5). The characteristic that these cases share is a stair that irregularly consumes a portion of an otherwise coherent room. Occasionally, the stair formally treats the entire central bay as a stair hall (fig. 2.6). In still other villas, an anomalous narrow bay filled with the stair is inserted between a side bay and the main hall (fig. 2.7-overleaf). This solution preserves the identical dimension of the three primary bays but compromises the symmetry of the entire ensemble.

As if on a par with matters of proportion, bilateral symmetries make their appearance at Villa Tauro according to vicissitudes of perception and expectation. Like anamorphosis, the symmetry one sees at Tauro depends upon how one looks at it (fig. 2.8-overleaf). Optically contingent, it flickers in and out of focus. Depending on which elements are seen as primary, each symmetry begets or conceals another. Theoretically, such symmetry is extraneous to the

2.6 Villa Valduga, Feltre, Pren, 18th century.

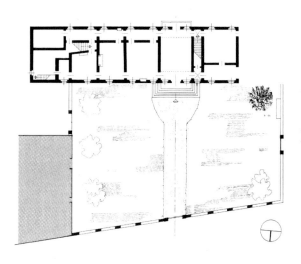

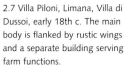

2.7 Villa Piloni, Limana, Villa di Dussoi, early 18th c. The main body is flanked by rustic wings and a separate building serving farm functions.

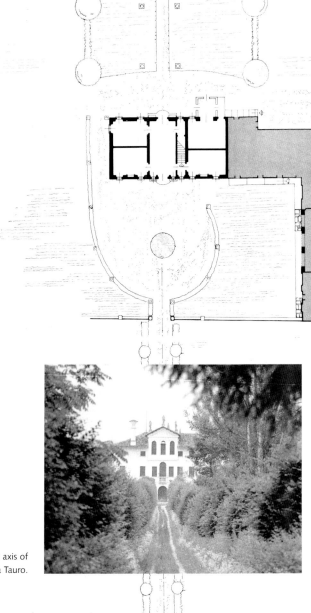

2.8 The off-center axis of Villa Tauro.

32

seventeenth-century concept of symmetry as defined by Claude Perrault (1613–88). Perrault identified bilateral symmetry as an absolute category of beauty. He separated and distinguished it from arbitrary sources of beauty, including proportion. This differed radically from the Albertian conception of proportion that rested on *concinnitas*—the harmonious relationship of part to whole—and implied bilateral symmetry.[2] In the unique context of Venice, before the appearance of the post-Bramantean *all'antica* style beginning under the reign of Doge Andrea Gritti, bilateral symmetry was determined empirically.[3] The tripartite with each part being equal was indifferent to hierarchy and *a priori* proportional systems and thus prefigured Perrault's positive bilateral symmetry, which presupposed an empiricist approach to proportion.

What distinguishes Villa Tauro's façade from Cad'Oro, Palazzo Mocenigo. and other façades analyzed by Colin Rowe and Peter Eisenman, is that it does not rely as much on overlapping vertical rows of windows (laterally overlapped patterns of symmetry) as it does on overlapping horizontal bands and varying degrees of continuity and discontinuity between them.[4] Take, for example, the tripartite series fused with the quadripartite series on the ground and second floors. It widens on the third floor where it is included in the cinquepartite system. The shift between second and third floors implies a division between them that remains otherwise unarticulated. In another case, the approximate cinquepartite system includes windows only on the third and second floors, suggesting a division between the second and first floors where the cinquepartite pattern terminates.

Finally, though, unlike other facades that exhibit multiple symmetries, Tauro's—with its horizontal discontinuities—makes explicit a characteristic of Venetian palaces that is specifically conditioned by the city. In the early sixteenth century, Venetian palaces began to feature stacked *piani nobili*, a horizontal stratification that denied vertical hierarchy (fig. 2.9). This dissolution of hierarchy in palaces was initiated by increased land values and density, among other demands of the city. In contrast to the necessities sponsored by the city, the horizontal repetition found in country villas was a product of typological inheritance, habit, or mimicry. Villa Tauro is exceptional because its manner of horizontal stacking neither replicates the palatial sources nor is necessitated by the city. Rather, it is presumably attributable to another imperative: to preserve the tripartite system while simultaneously adhering to a modest plan absorbing an extraneous stair bay. The resulting horizontal breaks

on the façade strengthen vertical connections maintained elsewhere. Thus, Tauro's stratification is an intensified version of that which occurs in other country villas and Venetian palaces. The predicament of concealing the stair within the equal tripartite system compelled Tauro's architect to take exception with the normative horizontal pattern of its Venetian antecedents. The consequence is that Tauro ultimately refers more vigorously to the Venetian urban condition than do its countryside counterparts.

Notes

1. Ennio Concina, *A History of Venetian Architecture*, Judith Landry trans. (New York: Cambridge University Press, 1998), 173–236.

2. For more about the bifurcation of Albertian Concinnitas, the split between bilateral symmetry as an aspect of positive beauty and proportion as arbitrary beauty, see Claude Perrault, *Ordonnance for the Five Kinds of Columns After the Method of the Ancients*, Harry F. Mallgrave, ed. (Los Angeles: The Getty Center for the History of the Humanities, 1993), 47–63; and Hanno-Walter Kruft, *A History of Architectural Theory From Vitruvius to the Present* (New York: Princeton Architectural Press, 1994), 134–5.

3. Concina, *Venetian Architecture*, 173–236.

4. Colin Rowe and Robert Slutzky, "Transparency: Literal and Phenomenal Part II," *Perspecta* 13/14 (1971): 291–3; and Peter Eisenman, "The Futility of Objects," *Harvard Architectural Review* 3 (Cambridge, MA: MIT Press, 1984).

33

2.9 Venetian Palazzi.

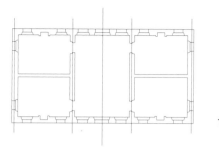

1

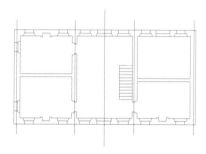

2

Diagrams 1–3

In Villa Tauro, two dominant interior walls suggest a tripartite organization. The added bay, which contains the stair, seems either to be located inside the central bay or to be inserted between the entrance hall and the right side bay. On the one hand, the width of the entrance hall together with the stair bay equals that of the side bays, suggesting that the stair is clearly contained within the central bay. On the other hand, the placement of the front door makes the *androne/portego* bay symmetrical, complete unto itself, and anomalous, appearing to have been squeezed to accommodate the added stair bay (compare diagrams 3 and 5). The result, in either interpretation, is that the tripartite system can be preserved, superficially at least, on the exterior. Ultimately, the fact that the stair prevents the realization of complete bilateral symmetry is, on the façade, nearly camouflaged. The additional bay of apertures associated with the stair belongs exclusively neither to an anomolous bay, to the central bay, nor to the side bay.

34

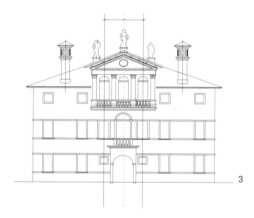

3

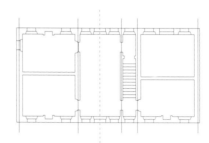

4

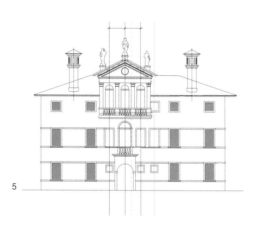

5

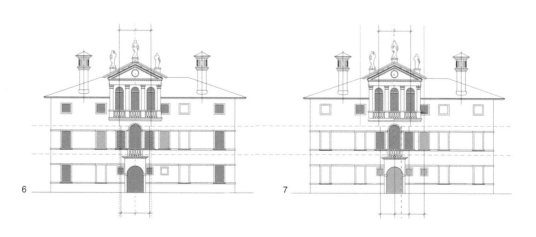

6

7

Diagrams 4–7

The effect of the added bay oscillating between zones has further implications for the perceived roles of other vertical rows of windows. From the exterior edges of the façade working inward, for example, the two side bays, each of which maintains a pair of widely set windows and a locally centralized chimney, are symmetrical. But the four remaining central rows of windows elude stable reference. That which defines the quadripartite division on the ground floor, with its center between rows rather than within one, is denied from the top down. Above, the pediment marks out only three bays as symbolically central, leaving the additional bay to the right of the tripartite series as an anomaly—an apparent insertion between the side and central bays. For these reasons, each floor oscillates between the absolute symmetry of equal dimensions and apparent symmetry based on the similarity of shape and the estimable positions of elements.

An alternative presents itself if the façade is scanned centrifugally. The pediment is embraced by two small windows that extend the tripartite group into a recognizable, albeit imperfect, cinquepartite series. Since one of the two small windows belongs to the stair bay, the bay to the immediate right of the stair bay now seems to be the anomaly. Thus the fusion of the tripartite, quadripartite, and cinquepartite series disguises the anomalous bay as normal and the normal bay as anomalous.

3

Elliptical Congruencies: The Tubular Embrasure of San Carlo ai Catinari

3.1 Façades of the Sacristy of San Carlo ai Catinari, at the intersection of Via del Monte della Farina and Via di S. Anna in Rome.

At the Sacristy of San Carlo ai Catinari in Rome, there is an astonishing episode hidden between what appear to be two separate windows; a cylindrical void, passing behind an exterior pilaster, pierces the corner of the building (fig. 3.1). What is difficult to discern, and can only be understood by comparing the interior to the exterior, is that there exists a very short passage linking an elliptical window on the inside of the sacristy to the side of the piercing cylinder (figs. 3.2 & 3.3). Thus, the two apertures on the facades pass light to a single interior window. The entire episode not only escapes visual notice, but also eludes the conventional definition of an embrasure (a direct passage, through a wall, from an interior and/or exterior opening to a window or a door).

Though the cylinder provides an effective source of diffuse light on the interior, it is not the most efficient means to this end. It would not be necessary if the exterior corner were parallel or slightly skewed relative to the diagonal interior wall or if the window were translucent or of stained glass. It seems particularly odd that an embrasure was deployed under circumstances that normally would prohibit it. The most obvious solution—a passage extending directly from the interior diagonal wall—was precluded as it would have maintained the integrity of one element—the

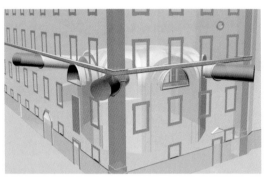

3.4 Hypothetical origin showing extruded embrasure violating the corner pilaster.

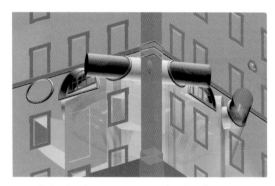

3.5 Cylindrical embrasure piercing two façades after rotation.

3.2 Elliptical interior window on the northwest corner.

3.3 Detail of the north façade.

embrasure—by destroying that of another, the exterior corner pilaster. The intersection of the two elements would be an unruly display of error, revealing the interior and exterior of the building to be incompatible derivatives of independent architectural motives. Thus, the staging and the avoidance of this taboo created a hybrid between an element within classical architecture (an embrasure or a bifurcated embrasure) and a form outside it (a cylindrical tube/void).

Similarly inconspicuous and exceptional is the geometry of the tube's identical apertures, which symmetrically flank the corner pilaster. Initially, they seem to be ovals, a motif common in baroque Rome. In fact, they are ellipses, the eccentricity of which calibrates the position of the cylinder with the idiosyncratic angle between the streets, the diagonal interior corner and multiple symmetrical and serial patterns of fenestration (see diagram 6). As opposed to the oval, which is a combinatory two-dimensional shape, the ellipse implies the presence of a system auxiliary to architecture: projective geometry. This association is particularly convincing if the ellipses are considered to be strictly geometrical results rather than proper elements of classicism. Among other aims, projective geometry seeks to identify congruent and invariant properties belonging to multiple sections of geometri-

cal primitives. If the façades of the sacristy are likened to cutting planes or planes of projection, the ellipses becomes equivalent to sections or traces (intersections) of various cylinders and cones. This provides an alternative explanation for ellipses otherwise construed by architectural historians as baroque motifs and frequently mistaken for ovals.[1] Thus, projective geometry, as a point of departure, leads to the reassessment of two key elements in architecture—the embrasure and the ellipse.

In the context of the sacristy, projective geometry can be understood to be the protagonist in a dynamic process precipitated by architectural motives and prohibitions. Such a process can begin, for example, with the elliptical windows extruded along axes normal (perpendicular) to the diagonal corners of the interior (fig. 3.4); while two windows interrupt existing symmetrically disposed ellipses on the exterior, another creates the forbidden intersection with the external corner, giant-order pilaster. Something has to yield. In the metamorphic process that follows, the embrasure can be hypothesized to rotate (fig. 3.5). The subsequent establishment of congruency among all the elliptical openings in the facades requires other rotations that, while ensuring unity, simultaneously disrupt several other discrete systems of regulatory order

3.6 Corner view.

38

(symmetry, seriality, coaxiality) in such a way that they become inextricably interlocked. The result is a rotated embrasure that, though an anomalous tube, is nevertheless deftly rendered homologous to the established norm from which it deviates. The anomaly, having caused the disruption of the very systems that govern the distribution of normative elements, thereby produces a more elaborate and encompassing combinatory order.

In short, architectural codes of decorum forbid an embrasure from intersecting, much less burrowing through, a classical corner pilaster, and a geometrical narrative ensues when the embrasure becomes a cylinder that rotates in order to avoid such an intersection. Thus, an architectural predicament is established: the need for an embrasure at the corner arises; the geometry of this architectural element suggests an unacceptable solution (the perpendicular extrusion of an embrasure and its intersection with a corner pilaster); and this is resolved through a series of preventative nonarchitectural geometric processes (the first of which is the rotation of the cylindrical embrasure away from the corner and its double intersection with the façades). The assumed acts of rotation and intersection make evident that the tube piercing the building is a symptom of an architectural taboo.

Rarity, Adaptation, Co-optation

The inquiry into anomalies can be considered within its own history, that of wonder. From early medieval to modern times, to speak of wonder has meant to speak of rarity.[2] In their book *Wonders and the Order of Nature*, Lorraine Daston and Katharine Park point out that in the mid-seventeenth century (at the time of the sacristy's construction), 'wonder' referred both to the passions of inquiry into hidden causes and into natural and artificial objects.[3] Such objects were revered for their novel singularity in defiance of utility or unitary identity. They ranged from exotica (coral branches, giant emeralds, a two handled fork) to anatomical rarities (hermaphrodites, a skeleton fused with two joints, a man without any sense of taste) to artistic virtuosity (ivory turned to web-like thinness, painted miniatures). Many of the most significant examples represented a hybrid between art and nature. Marvelous natural oddities, seen by natural philosophers as indications of nature's inventiveness in overcoming material flaws, were likened to the works of a clever artisan who invents exceptional forms in order to transgress material recalcitrance. They were prized not only by natural philosophers but revered among collectors who, in displaying them together with artificial objects of curiosity, sought to reinforce the

3.7 Athanasius Kircher, "listening cone" from Musurgia Universalis (see footnote 5).

equation of the artificial and the organic.

Though the notion of wonder was associated with baroque architecture, as Joseph Connors writes, it primarily referred to either visual displays of geometrical virtuosity or delightful optical devices (such as mirrors or painted anamorphoses) applied to the main body of architecture.[4] It did not fixate upon rare exceptions within the classical language of architecture that were not overtly spectacular. Though the tube is arguably rare (there are no known comparable examples) it is not due to its spectacularity but to the way in which it ingeniously overcame the binding limits of a system of form by concealing itself within it. In this way it is more like natural and other artificial wonders of the seventeenth century than it is wondrous as architecture. Questions concerning the categorization of singular or unique objects were salient to the curious—a winged cat could be classified as bird or mammal, coral as animal or mineral—and the tube similarly straddles categorical boundaries; as an open air passage without a thermal barrier, the tube subverts the definition of an embrasure and appears to cross it with that of another form, a listening cone—regardless of the disparity between the visual and acoustical functions of the two.[5] (fig. 3.7) Nevertheless, since concealment rather than visually accessible architectural virtuosity

accounts for the ingenuity of the tube, it probably did not arouse curiosity.[6]

The tube is not primarily a response to function, but instead to the necessity for the classical language to adapt. Fortuitously, as the classical language mutates in the sacristy, the tube transmits even stealthier and more beautifully diffuse light than would a more conventional embrasure. This kind of perverse functionalism—in which the adaptation of form was not seen as fundamentally necessary (even at times excessive) for an essential function but was nevertheless considered to produce "more beautiful" results than a normative form— was, according to Daston and Park, particular to an early modern (eighteenth-century) view of wonder as it regarded the marvel of monstrous births. Exceptions such as a woman with two wombs (who gave birth to two separate very healthy children) or the supple ligament that replaced the pelvic bone and facilitated the independent movements of twins conjoined at the hip, were admired by anatomists because they functioned even "more usefully" than their "more usual" counterpart. Oddities in this sense were no longer admired for their singularity (or were no longer of interest in themselves), but exemplified malformations that, because they were explained in terms of function, could be considered extraordinary (rather

40

3.8 Flatfish.

3.9 Pablo Picasso, *Portrait of Dora Maar*, 1937. Musee Picasso, Paris.

3.10 The asymmetrical west façade.

than naturally erroneous or novel) and thus revelatory of a more elaborate normative system. To the extent that the tube is perversely functional, it is—like the anatomical marvels of the eighteenth century—not aberrant, but extraordinary.

By the late eighteenth century, as nature had become increasingly normalized, rarities could not be seen as violations of natural law. Instead, they were recognized as deviations from the customary. A marvel as such was no longer considered rare universally, but rather perceived as "other," that is, rare only in relation to another norm. In other words, rarity was redefined in relative terms, with the strange and the familiar perceived only according to convention or habit.[7] Such a shift from the natural sciences to the realm of the social can perhaps best be clarified through a case of adaptation regular in nature. The flatfish, for example, is a fish whose compressed body adapts, during an early stage of development, to the need to eat and live

at the bottom of the sea. It mutates in overall form and structure such that one eye moves to the same side of the body as the other. The fish then swims with its eyeless side down (fig. 3.8). The head of such a fish appears distorted because most of its body retains a structure resembling more numerous aquatic vertebrates whose eyes, pectoral fins and mouth remain symmetrical. What would appear either as profile or front on other fish appears as both conflated on the flatfish. The simultaneity of views translated and flattened can be likened to Pablo Picasso's portraits of the late 1930s (fig. 3.9). But in the flatfish, since front and side collapsed together rotate to become top, the implication is that what were side and front elevations become plan.

The tubular embrasure, in contrast to cubism, is comparable to the flatfish in that it is the indirect result of an adaptive process. Moreover, the tube compares to the flatfish because it is distinguished as "other" and is fused with norms; the relationship between the tube and a more normative embrasure can be compared to that between the flatfish and a "normal" fish. Yet because the rarity of the tube is disguised within the classical language, it is, unlike the fish, an anomaly that appears normal yet functions perversely.

3.11 Street plan.

3.12 Plan of San Carlo ai Catinari.

The Sacristy at San Carlo ai Catinari: Chronology (figs. 3.11 & 3.12)

Prior to 1575, the site of San Carlo ai Catinari was occupied by a more modest church, San Biagio dall'Anello. In 1575, this church and nearby houses were acquired by the Barnabiti fathers, with the intention to construct a larger church. On 29 September 1611, the first stone for San Carlo was blessed and on 4 November ground was broken. By 26 February 1612, the chapel, by Gaspare Guerra, was completed. Construction under the direction of architect Rosato Rosati took place between 1612 and 1620, during which the nave was completed. Work on the façade's foundation was begun by G. B. Soria in January 1636 (Rosati died in 1625), and was completed two years later, in 1638. In 1636, chains were placed around the base of the cupola. Between 1638 and 1646 the apse was constructed and in 1650, the sacristy, choir, and rooms behind the apse were begun. A plan from the *Biblioteca Apostolica Vaticana* dates the building of the sacristy between 1650 and 1660.[8] By 17 April 1660, the Barnabites had built a quarter of the adjacent *convento*, but the attribution of the design of the sacristy to a particular architect is unresolved.

Notes

1. There are numerous occasions in which an oval has been mistaken for an ellipse. See, for example, Leo Steinberg, *San Carlo Alle Quattro Fontane: A Study in Multiple Form and Architectural Symbolism* (Ann Arbor, MI: University Microfilms, 1960), 147, n. 18, in which he discusses the geometry of coffers in the Palazzo Farnese.

2. The discussion of wonder that follows is largely based on Lorraine Daston and Katharine Park, *Wonders and the Order of Nature, 1150–1750* (New York: Zone Books, 1998), a text brought to my attention by Mirka Benes. See also discussions by Carlo Ginzburg, "The High and the Low: The Theme of Forbidden Knowledge in the Sixteenth and Seventeenth Centuries," in *Clues, Myths, and the Historical Method,* trans. John and Anne C. Tedeschi (Baltimore: Johns Hopkins University Press, 1989); and Kryzstof Pomian, *Collectors and Curiosities: Paris and Venice, 1500-1800,* trans. Elizabeth Wiles-Portier (Cambridge, MA.: Polity Press, 1990). Also pertinent is Foucault's introduction to Georges Ganguilhem, *The Normal and the Pathological* (New York: Zone Books, 1978).

3. Daston and Park, *Wonders,* 303–28.

4. Joseph Connors, "Virtuoso Architecture in Cassiano's Rome," in *Cassiano Dal Pozzo's Paper Museum* vol. 2 (Milan: Olivetto, 1992), 23–40; See also "Ars Tornadi: Baroque Architecture and the Lathe," *Journal of the Warburg and Courtauld Institutes* 53 (1990): 217–36, plates 22–8.

5. From Athanasius Kircher, *Musurgia Universalis* (Rome: ex typographia hearedum Francisci Corbelletti, 1650). This plate was brought to my attention by Daniel Sherer. The listening tube is an open-air funnel through which messages were to be inconspicuously spoken from the mouths of statues, passing from one room to another through a thick wall. Spiral or shell shaped, it resembles the inner ear.

6. Within the mid-seventeenth century, curiosity became inextricably "allied with wonder." While wonder "acted as bait for" and would capture curiosity, curiosity connoted, according to Hobbes, the insatiable "desire, to know why and how." Daston and Park, *Wonders,* 311–28.

7. "Monsters were 'animals whose deformities horrify,' but the horror sprang from violated convention, not violated nature." Daston and Park, *Wonders.* See also, Voltaire, "Monstres" from his "Dictionnaire philosophique," in *Oeuvres completes de Voltaire* vol. 20 (Paris: Garnier Freres, 1877–85), 108–9.

8. Primary documents and the most recent research regarding San Carlo ai Catinari is found in Valter Vannelli's "S. Carlo ai Catinari: Chiesa e Cupola in un Organismo Centrale con assi differenziati," in *Quaderni dell'Istituto di Storia dell'architettura* 15–20 (1990–92): 717–28.

3.13 Primary image used for façade reconstruction.

3.14 Cylindrical and conic embrasures

42

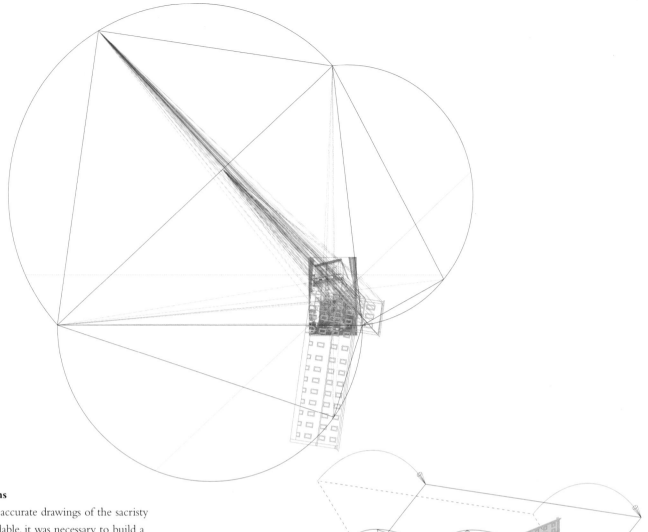

Diagrams

Since no accurate drawings of the sacristy
were available, it was necessary to build a
model based on photographs (figs. 3.16 &
3.17). The model was projected from the
photographs according to the Taylorian
method, which produces orthographic projections from perspectives (Taylorian
method is discussed at length in Chapter
4). The portions of the embrasures that
were not visually accessible to the author
or were not intelligible in the photographs
are, in the model, based on conjecture.
They have been idealized in order to support a hypothetical narrative based on the
aforementioned process of adaptation. It is
far from certain, for example, that the corner tube is based on a cylinder. The conic
embrasure is entirely speculative (fig. 3.15).

43

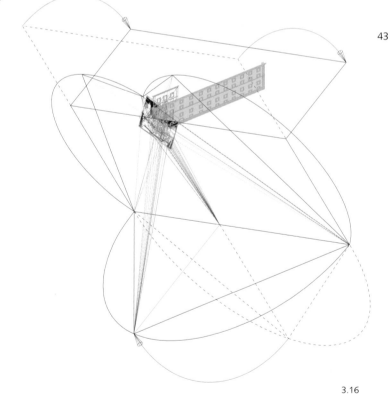

3.16

3.15

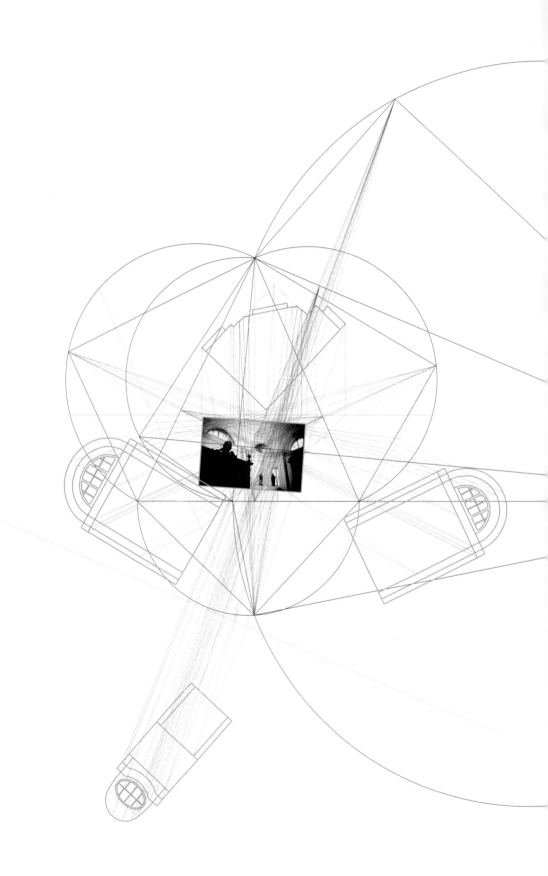

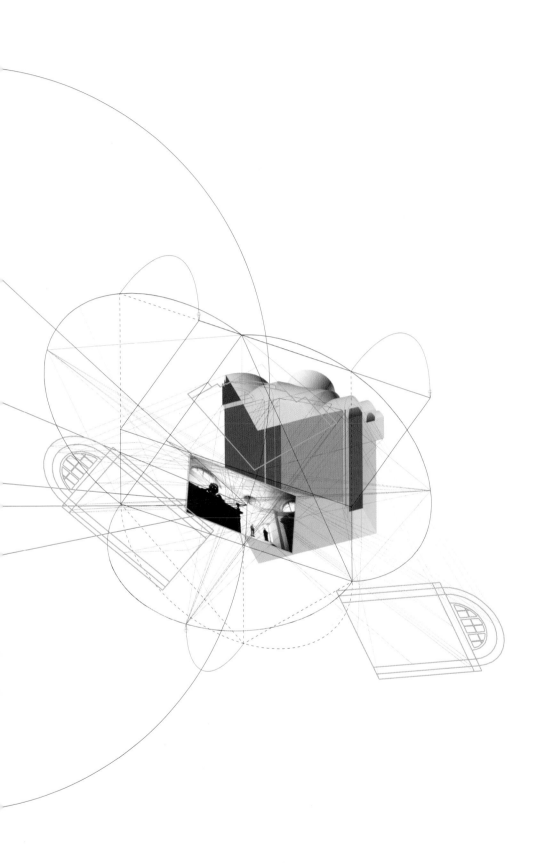

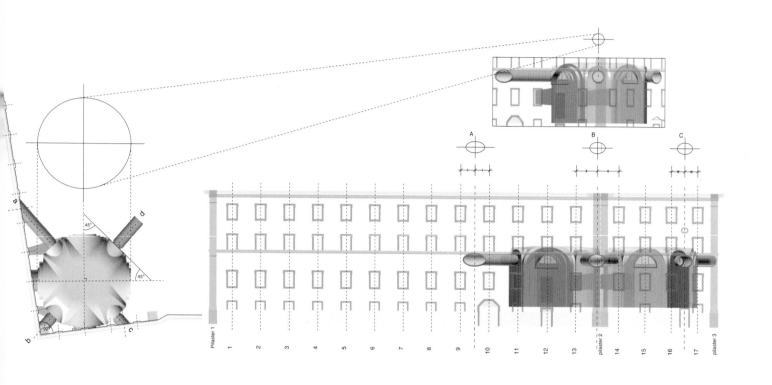

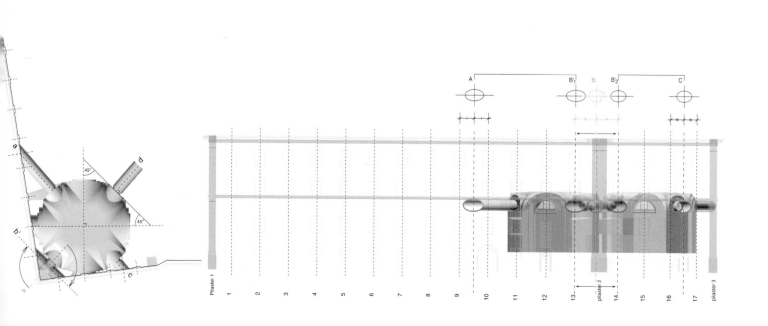

Diagram 1: A Three Part Hypothesis

The following investigation begins with the assumption that an anomaly in architecture—a tube serving as a passage for light—can be effectively explained by hypothetical organizational structures that are interlocked and altered in response to multiple inconsonant demands. Three organizations are proposed and combined. The first is derived from a substantial remnant of a serial pattern that covers two-thirds of the existing north façade. The second is established by a discrete symmetrical bay on the west façade uniquely annunciated by the presence of a tiny elliptical window. When the remnant on the north façade is extended, and the remnant on the west façade is repeated, the result is remarkably coherent; each fills and is centered within its respective façade. The two patterns can thus be assumed to establish a convincing point of departure.

The third organization results from the proportional readjustment of the existing interior in order that all three types of its window embrasures be commensurate with the proposed serial patterns of the north and west façades. The four elliptical windows extrude along axes perpendicular to the diagonal corners of the interior. They become embrasures that trans-

mit diffuse light, such that the intersections (ellipses *A* and *C*) of embrasures *a* and *c* with the facades lie centered within bays. *b* lies centered in the bay between the two façades when they are unfolded into a single plane but it does not lie on the centerline of the unfolded pilaster. *C* lies centered in the bay distinguished by the tiny elliptical window. Both the arcuated and rectangular embrasures fall into line with vertical rows of windows. The entire room remains aligned with the orthogonal coordinate system of the church. The four major walls of the sacristy and the interior walls of the mandible-like embrasures to the north always

remain parallel to the north-south axis of the room. Since the extruded elliptical embrasures are fixed by the façade, it is assumed that they should originate perpendicular to their respective chamfered corners. The angle of those corners is bound to be 45 degrees to the coordinate system of the church as determined by the proportional adjustment of the entire interior.

At this point, all of the extruded embrasures and angled corners of the interior are highly calibrated with respect to the now-complete serial patterns of the façades. What is striking about this three part hypothesis is that while it exhibits a high degree of

determinacy in terms of interdependent systems of order inside and out, it is predicated on an impermissible taboo: as the elliptical embrasures extrude perpendicularly from their respective interior diagonal walls, the exterior northwest corner pilaster is necessarily violated. Thus, it can be further hypothesized that although *b* was capable of transmitting diffuse light, the discordant circumstance it caused at the corner required it to rotate. (Apparently the integrity of the apse of San Carlo ai Catinari was non-negotiable and precluded any possibility of developing an embrasure on the southeast corner.)

47

Diagram 2: A Point of Rotation

The rotation of embrasure *b* occurs such that its axis becomes parallel to the 45 degree chamfered corner and its intersections with the north and west façades produce ellipses that fall into line with the vertical rows of windows flanking the corner pilaster. This requires the point on which *b* rotates to coincide with the intersection of the axis of *b* and the axis defined by a line passing through the center points of the two rows of windows flanking the corner pilaster. The intersection of *b'* with the north and west facades produces two different ellipses congruent with previously established elliptical sections, *A* and *C*. Thus *b'* produces the two sets *A* and *B1* on the north façade, and *B2* and *C* on the west façade.

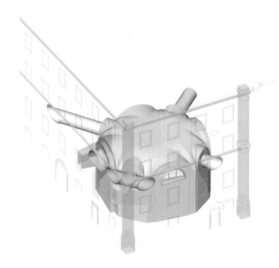

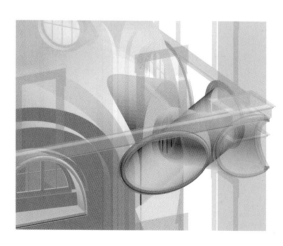

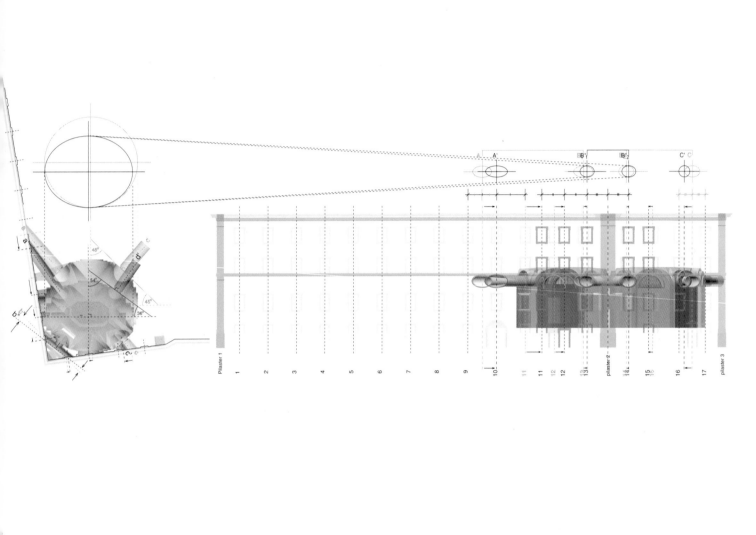

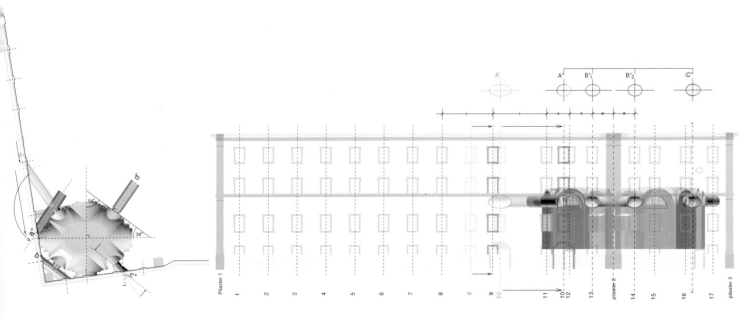

Diagram 3. Toward Congruency

The sacristy as built shows that all four elliptical intersections are destined to be congruent and proportionally congruent with a larger ellipse that corresponds approximately with the plan of the sacristy proper. In order for $B'1$ and $B'2$ to become congruent with each other as well as with the overall sacristy plan, b' must rotate. And since the axis of b' is bound by parallelism to the northwest chamfered corner, the room is scaled nonuniformly in order for that corner to become the angle of b' rotated (now b''). This angle produces elliptical intersections $B''1$ and $B''2$ congruent in their eccentricity with one another as well as with the squashed room. Resulting from this transformation are embrasures a', c', and d'.

An Additional Assumption

Once an elliptical intersection falls into line with a row of windows, it is assumed to be locked to that row. Either ellipse or row may move laterally provided that the other moves along with it. Upon the proportional adjustment of the sacristy interior, the arcuated and rectangular windows as well as $B''1$ and $B''2$ require rows 11 through 15 to shift in order to bring the fenestration of the west facade into concordance with the composition as built, with the exception of the elliptical intersection C'. Also required is the creation of the as built tripartite system on the north façade organized according to the final position of the arcuated opening.

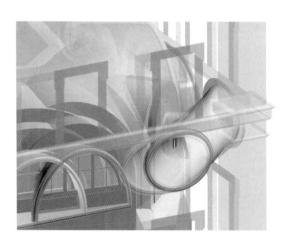

Diagram 4: A Failed Attempt

As an alternative, embrasure a' could rotate sharply toward the corner and create an ellipse A'' congruent with $B''1$, and $B''2$, while c' could rotate away from the corner and create congruent ellipse C''. This is a compelling possibility since it would create a pattern of tubes that emphasize the directional north/south axis of the sacristy. The result, however, is a violation of the arcuated window on the north façade even more unacceptable than the violation of the pilaster initiated by extruding embrasure b through the northwest corner pilaster. In addition, this rotation requires rows of windows 10 and 16 to break the fenestral organization without establishing alternative resolutions.

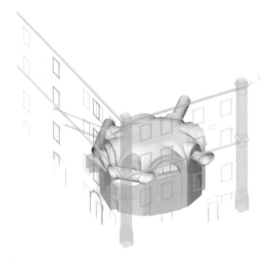

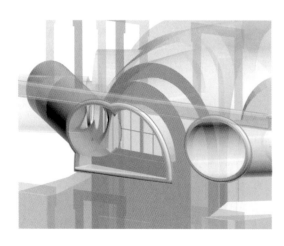

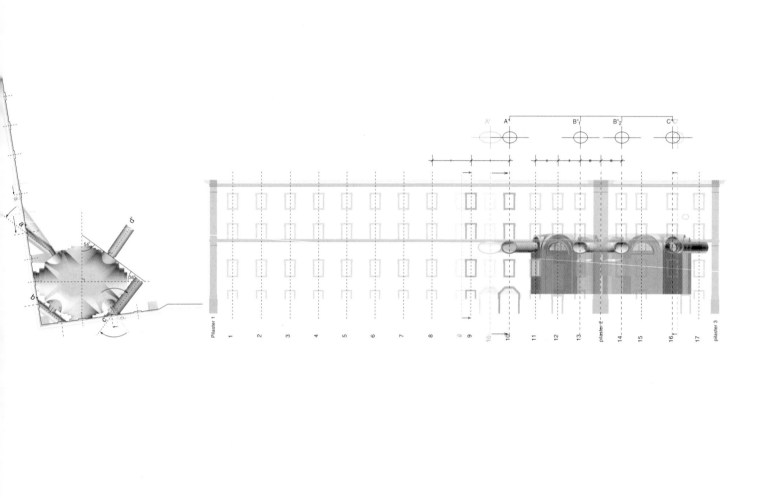

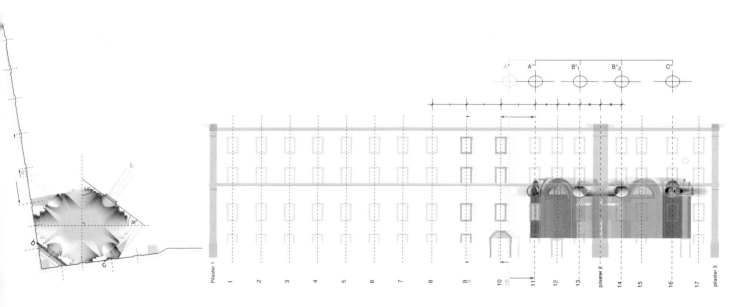

Diagram 5: Attaining Congruency
Congruency among all four elliptical intersections is achieved when a' and c' rotate from the same point relative to their respective diagonal walls as did b and b'. The angle of rotation is locked in by the attainment of congruency. The slight rotation of embrasure a' toward the corner creates an ellipse A" coaxial with a vertical row of windows (row 10) and thereby requires the row to shift laterally in the direction of the corner. The rotation of c' creates C" congruent with A", B"1, and B"2, and simultaneously becomes coaxial with a row of windows (row 16). This brings the fenestral composition of the west façade into correspondence with the built version.

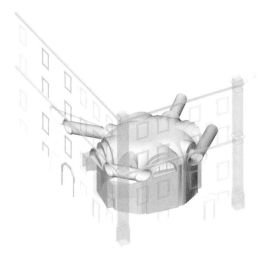

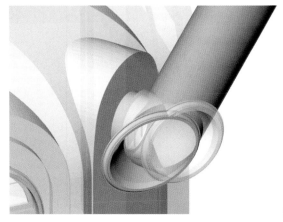

51

Diagram 6: The Tripartite Imperative and the Conic Embrasure
Though the first approach to bringing A' into congruency with the other three elliptical intersections might be optimal, there nevertheless follows another problem. The distance from both the rotation point and the window of a" to the facade is too great to sustain sufficient leverage or purchase. (Its length is also absurdly great relative to the need for reasonable diffuse light.) Thus, a" disappears and relinquishes its hold on the elliptical opening A" on the façade. This allows A" to sheer away from a" and relocate to a position coaxial with row 11. This resolves, with a single stroke, a multitude of fenestration problems that had stemmed from a holding onto its tenuous status as an embrasure. At this point, since the embrasure has utterly disappeared, the interior window becomes blind and thereby pairs with the other blind interior ellipse. There are now two pairs of elliptical windows inside: one pair is blind and the other open. By pairing off this way, the elliptical windows become related to the pairs of blind and open arcuated openings. On the façade, the window rows drift laterally into positions that establish a graduated transition between the

series 1–8 and the tripartite series 11–13. It is as if A" gives up the futile effort to sustain itself as the opening into an embrasure against all the opposing systems to which until now it had been beholden. By relinquishing its physical bond to the excessively attenuated embrasure a", A" becomes associated with the tripartite system and releases the tension that it had created in the façade. The molding that frames A"', though equal to that of the three other ellip-

tical openings with which it is congruent, now becomes an empty cameo applied to the utterly uninterrupted surface of the building. This is not, therefore, a blind window but rather an empty frame—an applique—that admits to its status as a disembodied relic or trace, a forged solution to the problems of congruency, coaxiality, and a concession to the fenestration pattern.

In the meantime c" undertakes to complete itself in the most extraor-

dinary fashion by transforming into a cone. Its union with the original c' creates the only intersection that passes through the pre-established point of rotation. This allows embrasure c to follow its final trajectory from the interior to the façade. The cone funnels from the small interior window embrasure to the larger exterior elliptical opening.

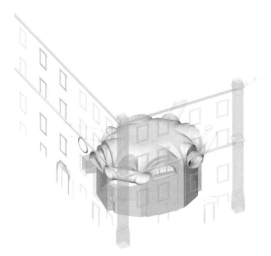

4
Inversive Projections: Taylorian Perspective Apparatus

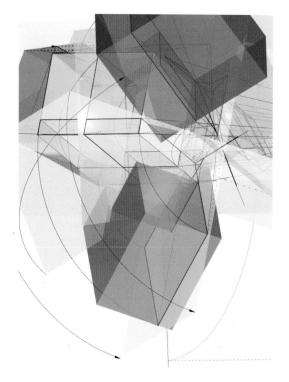

The process of distorting symmetry in order to flatten, as in the case of the flatfish, may be more aptly compared to an artifact auxiliary to architectural form: the three-dimensional projective apparatus of Brook Taylor, comprehensively described in axioms and demonstrated with two-dimensional diagrams and pictorial axonometric illustrations in his *Linear Perspective* of 1715 and *New Principles of Linear Perspective* of 1719.[1]

Unlike the villas and the sacristy, where compliance with principles of harmony and decorum leads to distortion, Taylor's apparatuses sponsor distortions that result from an unambiguous cause: the need to accurately translate three dimensions into two in order to create a verisimilitude of visual reality on a drawing surface. This procedure is neither conceived nor resolved empirically. Rather, it is related to the development of descriptive geometry. Based in part on projective geometry, descriptive geometry was codified by Gaspard Monge at the end of the eighteenth century.[2] It provides a two-dimensional means to represent three-dimensional elements and can be used to deduce not only projective but also metrical properties. In Monge's terms, three-dimensional elements are transferred to horizontal and vertical planes of projection. An intersection of an object (a line or a plane) with a plane of projection is called a trace. The planes of projection are then collapsed into a single two-dimensional surface.

In Taylor's method, the procedure that collapses three-dimensional objects and projections into two-dimensional plane surfaces serendipitously creates a type of distorted symmetry. The process by which three-dimensional operations of projection unfold into two dimensions requires reversing the object by rotating it relative to its perspective projection. When projected two dimensionally, this process links objects and perspectives of objects along a "ground line"—a line of intersection between the picture plane and a reference plane parallel to the horizon. Bound and reversed along this shared axis, it is possible to interpret the two projections of the object—one orthographic and the other perspectival—as mutually distorted and inverted versions of the same primary, three-dimensional object.

In the eighteenth century, the two-dimensional projection of a Taylorian perspective concealed the inversive procedure upon which it was based. The complete symmetry of the objects (i.e. of the buildings) that were projected made the inversive process appear inconsequential. Architectural symmetry effectively eclipsed the projective distortion of symmetry. In the cases presented here, however, the use of an asymmetrical object, coupled with three-dimensional computer modeling of Taylor's apparatuses, reveals a heretofore unrecognized method by which symmetry is regularly distorted.

Taylorian Two-Point Apparatus

A three-dimensional object and an eye position E in space serves as the foundation for an apparatus capable of producing a two-point linear perspective. The horizon plane (also called the vanishing plane) is located at the elevation of the eye. The picture plane is a plumb (vertical) plane inserted at an arbitrary location. In this case it is between the eye and the object. The front edge of the object, line segment JN, lies on the picture plane. A horizontal reference plane, or "ground plane," cuts through the object at an arbitrary location, yielding plan cut $GHIJ$. By definition, the groundplane and the horizon plane are parallel, and both are perpendicular to the picture plane.

Notes

1. For complete coverage of Taylor's theorems, see Kirsti Andersen, *Brook Taylor's Role in the History of Linear Perspective: A Study of Taylor's Role in the History of Perspective Geometry, Including Facsimiles of Taylor's Two Books on Perspective* (New York: Springer-Verlag, 1991).

2. For a thorough review of the principles of descriptive geometry, see William Henry Roever, *The Mongean Method of Descriptive Geometry* (New York: MacMillan, 1933)

Two-Point Perspective Apparatus with XY Vanishing Plane (XY Horizon Plane)

Diagram 1

The three-dimensional object and the eye *E* are doubly projected as in Mongian descriptive geometry. In this case, the picture plane serves as the vertical plane of projection while the ground plane coincides with the horizontal plane of projection. The vertical projection of the object is notated here as *A"C"M"K"* and the horizontal projection as *GHIJ* (*GHIJ* is coincident with *G'H'I'J'*—that is, with its horizontal projection).

Diagram 2

The three-dimensional system is flattened into two dimensions by revolving the eye point 90 degrees around horizon line *h,* the vertical trace of the horizon plane. The eye point revolved (*Er*) now lies in the picture plane. Similarly, the object is rotated 90 degrees around ground line *g,* such that the plane figure *GrHrIrJr* lies in the picture plane. The new horizontal projection *Ar'Cr'Mr'Kr'* remains identical to previous vertical projection *A"C"M"K"*. Plane figure *GHIJ*, on the other hand, is identical to *GrHrIrJr* in the three-dimensional

object(s), yet the projection in two dimensions presents them as inversions of one another. Together they produce a distorted symmetrical pair.

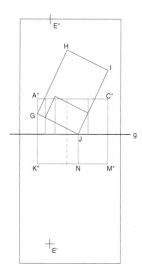

1

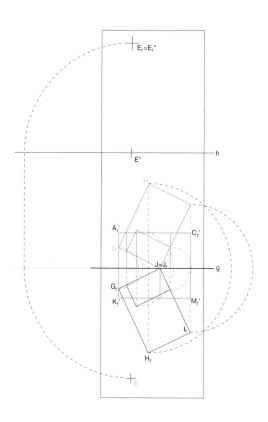

2

56

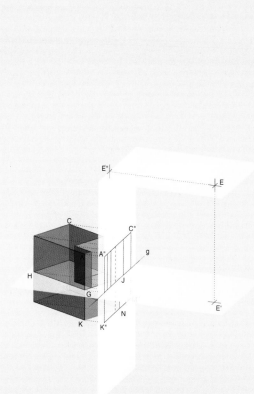

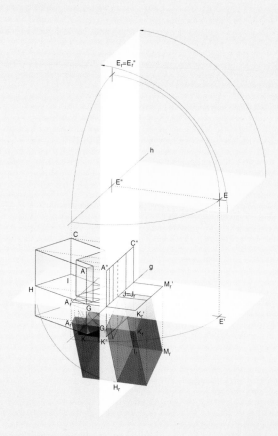

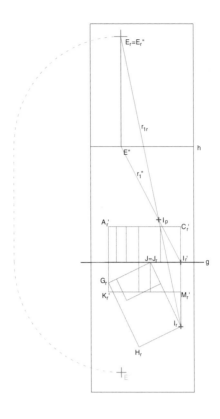

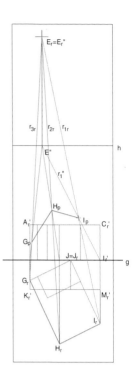

Diagram 3

The projection of line segment *r1* (a ray that connects an actual point on the object, *I*, with the actual eye point, E, is vertically projected as *r1"*). The intersection of line segment *r1"*, connecting *E"* and *Ir'* with the line segment connecting *Er* and *Ir*, gives the location in perspective of point *I*. This point *Ir* is coincident with the trace of ray *r1*, the location where the original ray *r1*—the ray connecting the three-dimensional eye point *E* and the three-dimensional point *I*—pierces the picture plane. It is as if the line connecting the three-dimensional *E* and the three-dimensional *I* (*r1r*) is elastic and remains connected to these points as they revolve about their respective axes.

Diagram 4

The process is repeated for every point in the plane figure of the object that lies in the ground plane revolved.

3

4

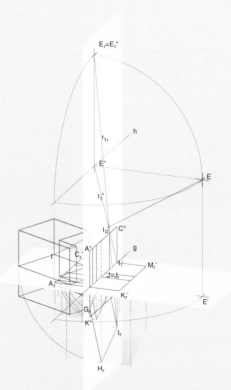

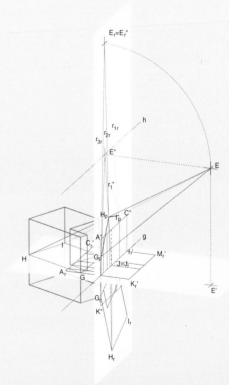

Diagram 5
Once all significant points of ground-plane cut *GHIJ* have been located in perspective, a distortion of the symmetry exhibited in diagram 2 is produced—i.e. the object projected and the perspective of the object projected create a distortion of the symmetry shown in diagram 2.

Diagram 6
Line segments connecting *E″* with *Cr′* and *Mr′* represent vertical projections of the three-dimensional rays connecting *E* to point *C* and *M* respectively. Because this two point machine does not account for vertical convergence, the perspective locations *Cp* and *Mp* are directly above and below *Ip*, respectively.

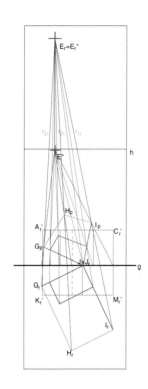

5

6

58

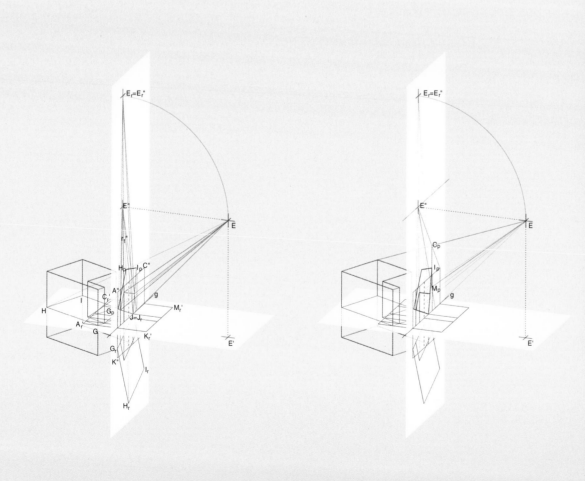

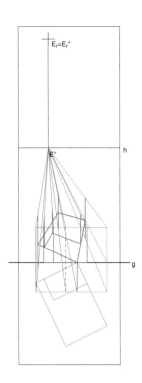

7

Diagram 7
Process in 6 repeats for all other vertical line segments.

Diagram 8
Object is rendered in perspective.

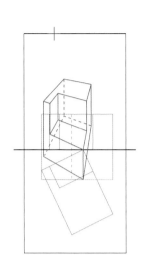

8

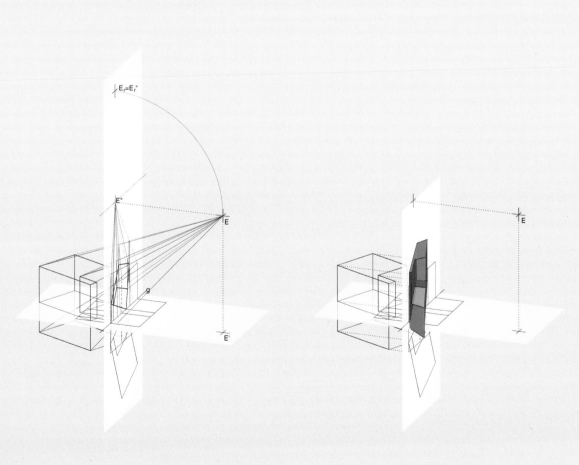

9

10

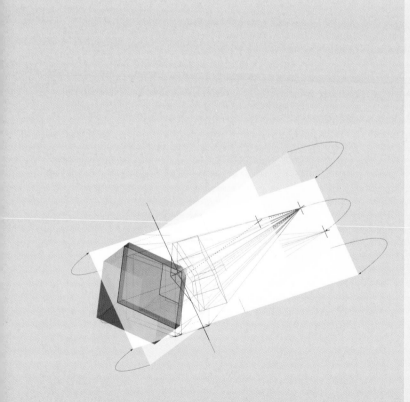

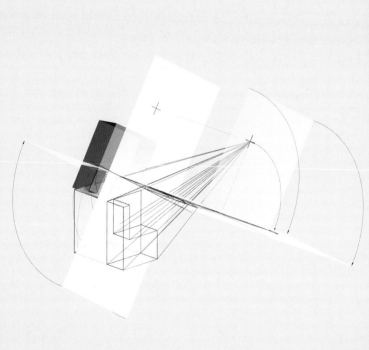

Diagram 9
Two-Point Perspective Apparatus
with *yz* vanishing plane (*yz* horizon
plane)

Diagram 10
Two-Point Perspective Apparatus
with *xz* vanishing plane (*xz* horizon
plane)

Diagram 11
Three two-point apparatuses shown
simultaneously, with vanishing planes
xy, *yz*, and *xz*, sharing the same eye
point

11

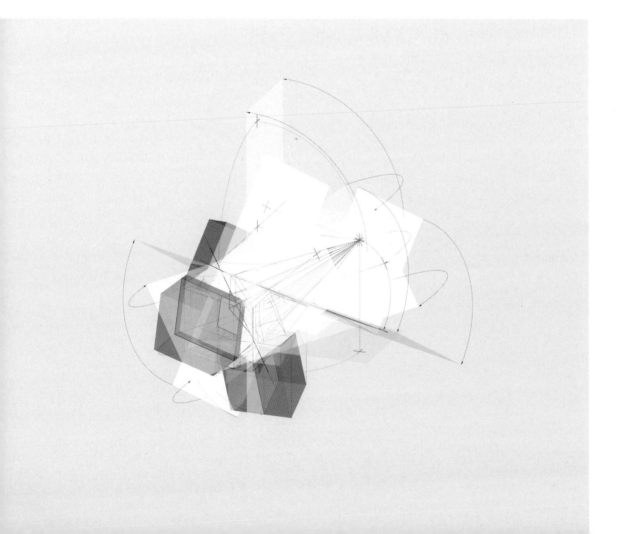

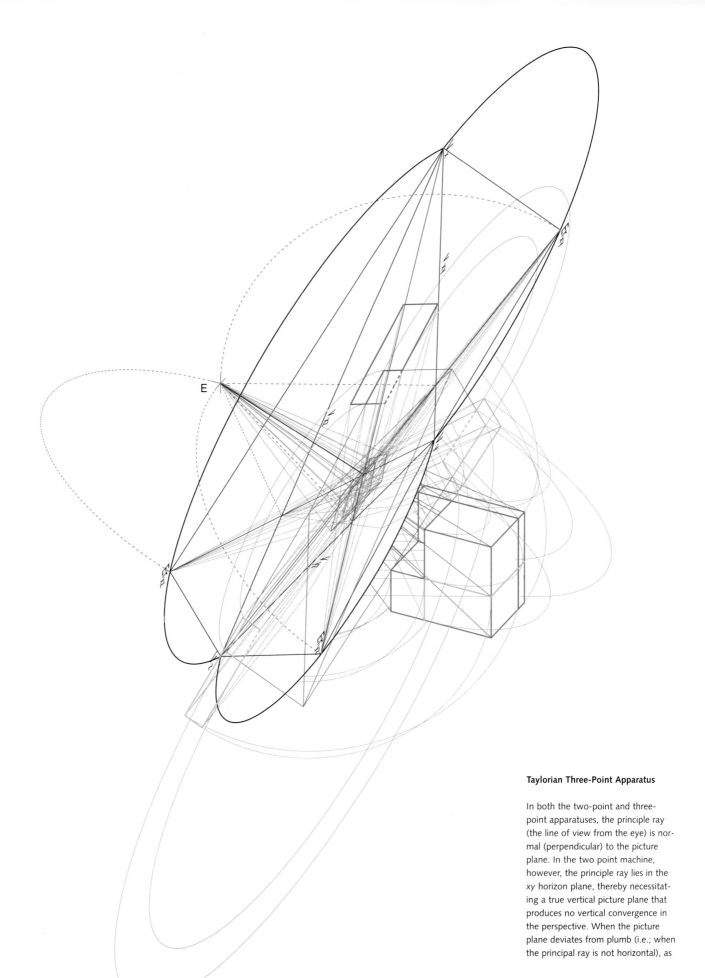

62

Taylorian Three-Point Apparatus

In both the two-point and three-point apparatuses, the principle ray (the line of view from the eye) is normal (perpendicular) to the picture plane. In the two point machine, however, the principle ray lies in the *xy* horizon plane, thereby necessitating a true vertical picture plane that produces no vertical convergence in the perspective. When the picture plane deviates from plumb (i.e.; when the principal ray is not horizontal), as

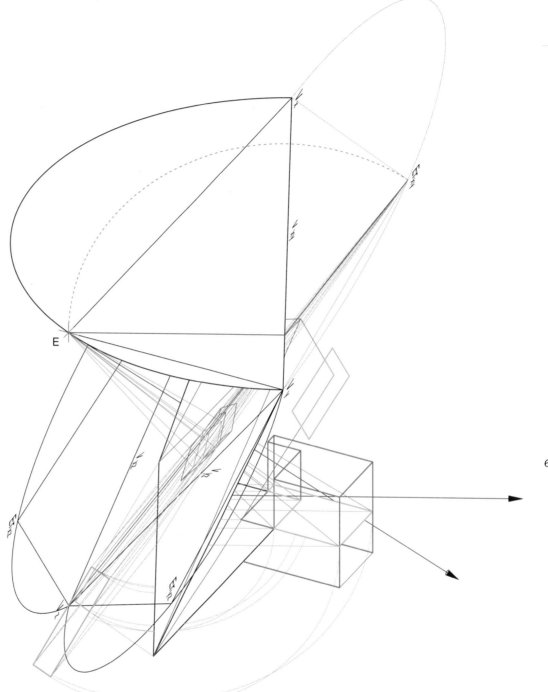

63

it does in the three-point machine, vertical convergence (perspective in the z axis) is accounted for.

The lack of a perpendicular relationship between the horizon plane and the picture plane creates two major procedural distinctions in the three-point machine: first, the angle of revolution for the eye point around the horizon line and the ground plane figure of the object around the ground line, cannot be equal to 90 degrees whereas in the two-point machine, they are always 90 degrees.

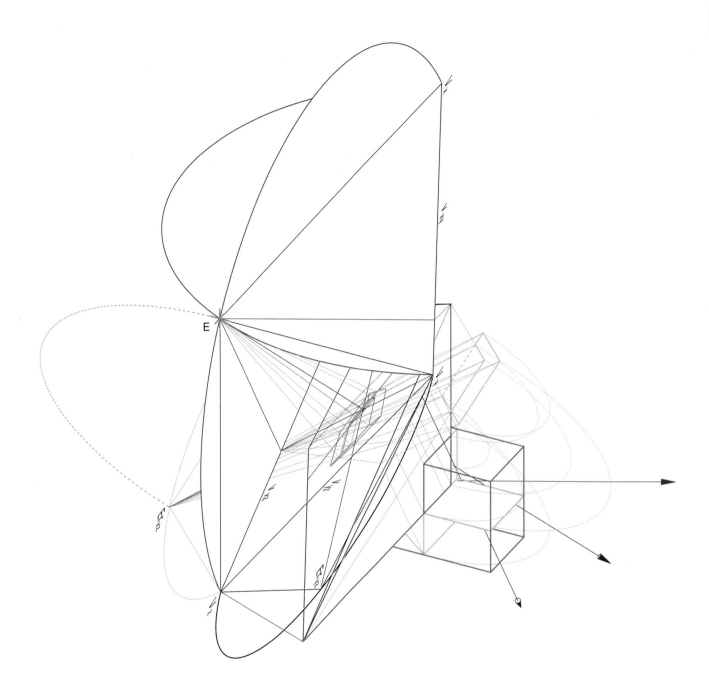

64

In the three-point case shown here, the angles of revolvement are obtuse.

Secondly, the three-dimensional rays connecting the eye and the points on a given ground plane figure, must be projected parallel to their correspondent vanishing plane and thus not perpendicularly to the picture plane. The three-point apparatus does not correspond to orthogonal projection—i.e.; Mongian double projection in that the projected rays used in the secondary geometry (in the two dimensional framework)

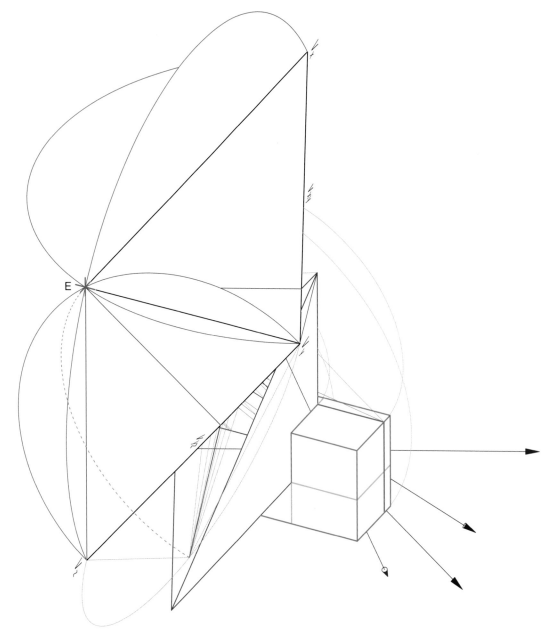

result from oblique projections.

In another operational distinction, to gain a complete perspective in the three-point apparatus, it is necessary to determine points in perspective with respect to all three vanishing planes *xy*, *xz*, and *yz*. The two-point machine, by ignoring one axis of convergence, actually omits two of the three vanishing planes.

Two Dimensional Diagrams of Three-Point Apparatus

(Lines entitled with the prefix *v* refer to vanishing planes and/or lines)

Diagram 1
Perspective of object

Diagram 2
Lines extended along each of three axes in perspective converge on three vanishing points: V_x, V_y, and V_z.

Diagram 3
Line v_{xy} (intersection of vanishing plane xy with picture plane) connecting V_x and V_y. This line represents the vanishing line for all plane figures parallel to the xy vanishing plane. A line drawn from V_z perpendicular to v_{xy} represents the principle ray p obliquely projected onto the picture plane and will be called p''_{xy}. The intersection of p''_{xy} with v_{xy} locates the oblique projection of the eye E''_{xy} along the xy vanishing plane. By extending p''_{xy} to intersect with a semicircle whose diameter is line segment v_{xy}, we locate the eye revolved with respect to $xy(Er_{xy})$. Again, the angle of revolvement is greater than 90 degrees.

A ground line g_{xy} is struck at an arbitrary location parallel to v_{xy}. This line represents the trace of the xy ground plane on the picture plane.

Diagram 4
Locating an orthogonal projection of a point lying in xy ground plane. A line segment is drawn from E''_{xy} to I_p and continues until it intersects the ground line g_r1'' is the oblique projection of three-dimensional ray r1 connecting three-dimensinal points E and I. In the two-dimensinal diagram, a line projected straight down from I''_{xy} is the oblique projection of arcs tracing the path of I to I_r. The place where this projection of the arc intersects with $r1_r$ (the elasticly projected three-dimensional ray) is the first point of a plane figure lying in the xy ground plane belonging to an orthogonal projection Ir_{xy}.

1

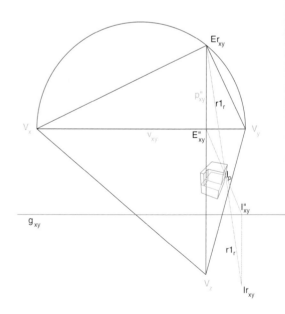

3

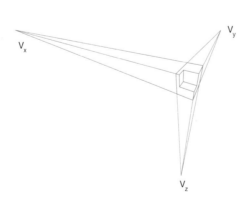

2

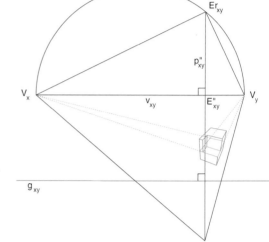

4

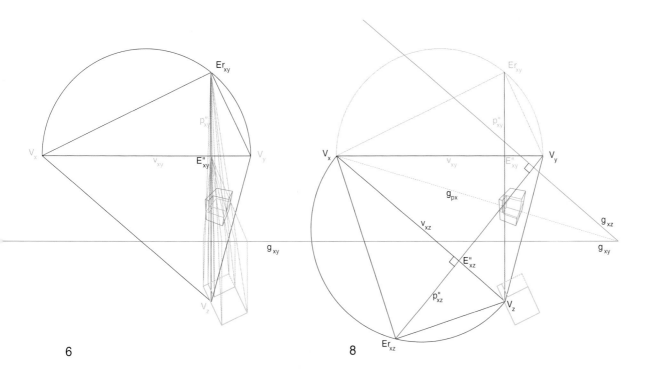

Diagram 5
Repeat diagram 4 to locate the orthogonal projection of two other points on the *xy* plane figure.

Diagram 6
Repeat operations of diagram 4 to obtain remaining *xy* points.

Diagram 7
Repeat diagram 3 for *xz* plane. Locate v_{xz}, Er_{xz}.

Diagram 8
Identification of ground line for *xz* plane figure. Line of intersection g_{px} (in perspective) of two ground planes—*xy* and *xz*—extended to intersect ground line g_{xy} (g_{px} is both an orthogonal and a perspective projection of the actual line of intersection between *xy* and *xz*). From this point of intersection, a line is struck that is parallel to v_{xz}. This line is the new ground line g_{xz}. This time, the location of the ground line (for *xz* and later for *zy*) is not arbitrary. It must be in this location in order for the second orthogonal projection of a second plane figure—this time lying in *xz*—to be the same scale as the first plane figure projected (lying in *xy*, as shown in diagrams 4–6).

5

7

6

8

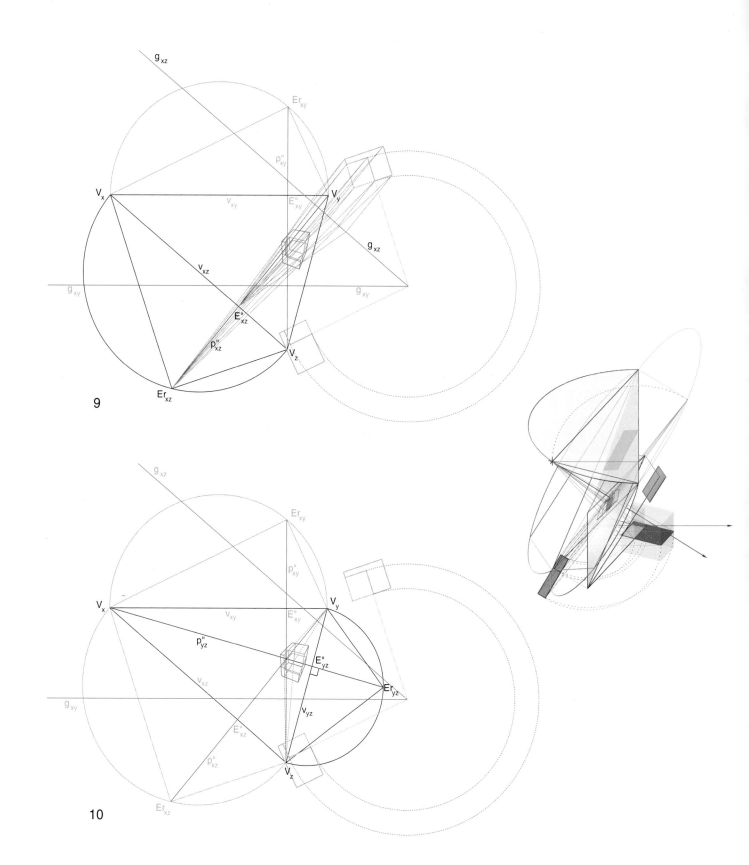

g_{xz}

Er_{xy}

p''_{xy}

V_x v_{xy} E''_{xy} V_y

g_{xz}

v_{xz}

g_{xy} g_{xy}

E''_{xz}

p''_{xz}

V_z

Er_{xz}

9

68

g_{xz}

Er_{xy}

p''_{xy}

V_x v_{xy} E''_{xy} V_y

p''_{yz}

E''_{yz}

v_{xz} Er_{yz}

g_{xy}

v_{yz}

E''_{xz}

p''_{xz} V_z

Er_{xz}

10

Diagrams 9–12
Revolutions and connections between
orthographic projections of the three
plane figures lying in the vanishing
planes *xy, yz,* and *xz.*

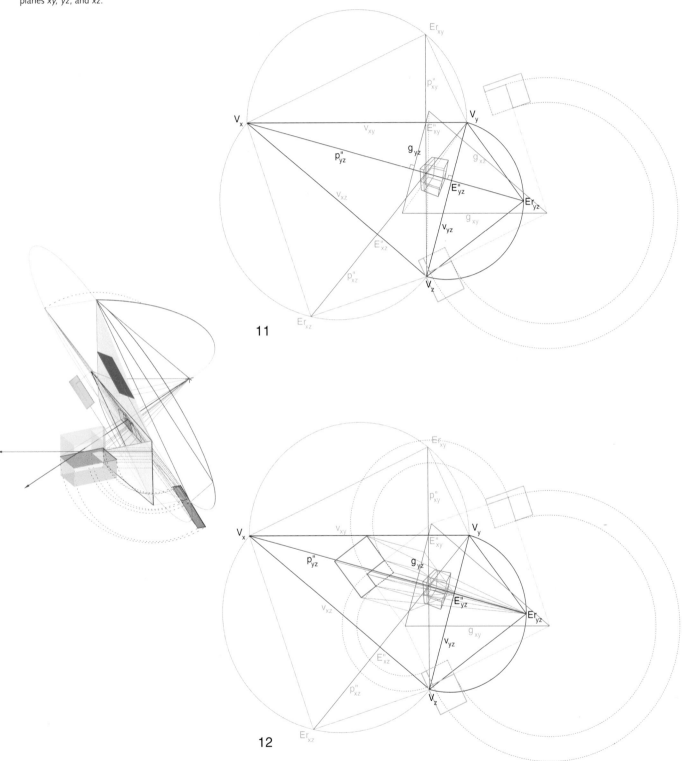

5
Projects

HOUSE ON LONGBOAT KEY, FLORIDA

Initial design: 1985–87

Redevelopment and construction documents: 1992

Two local ordinances exacerbate the contestations among symmetries in this house: the requirements that there be a pitched roof and that the main living areas be elevated in order to insure protection from flooding caused by hurricanes.

Since the 1970s on the Florida Gulf Coast Keys, most developers have insisted on concealing a significant portion of the ground floor of houses by adding sloped grounds. The rolling turf of high end Floridian suburban developments often looks like grass-covered dunes or picturesque golf courses. This house, on the other hand, maintains and addresses a completely flat site. It is more indebted to villas that refer to the water-threatened city of Venice than to English picturesque landscapes.

The house evolved from a conventional suburban split level type that has been rotated 90 degrees relative to the street. Or, it can be interpreted as the result of two linear volumes, each with a chevron-like façade and side elevation, that have been superimposed perpendicularly. The side of the larger of the two volumes faces the street and merges with the

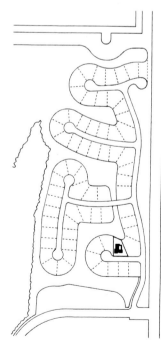

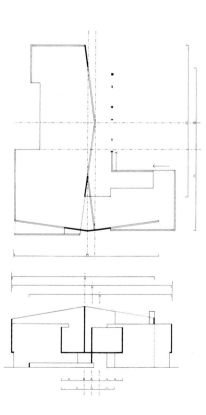

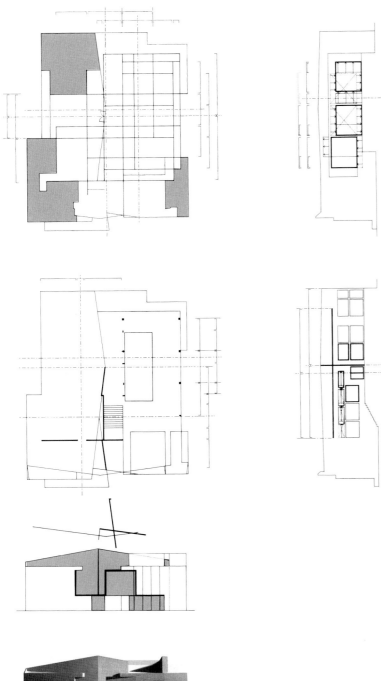

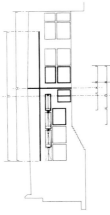

front of the narrower volume. Profile and frontal aspects are thus simultaneously affirmed and denied.

The doubling of the chevron façade is reinforced by the entry sequence. The threshold is a passage that recalls an *androne*. It bifurcates the ground plan and serves as a hall to a stair. The "true front," the second façade of the house, flanks the breezeway that extends beyond the *androne* stair. This front faces the pool that otherwise seems to be 'out back'. The internalized façade shears the ramp and grid, in plan and section, resulting in the split-level type organization. The shear marks a shift in the direction of circulation and separates two L-shaped groups of columns, symmetrically reversed. Opposite ends of the L's are aligned with their respective windows, but, contextually, they are inverted; one is inside the window of the first living room, the other is outside the window of the second and is located on a terrace raised relative to the pool. An apparently 'stra'" column in the entrance area, pinned by the angled wall, confirms that the symmetrical L's belong to a larger system of spatial punctuation points.

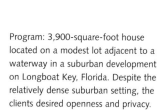

Program: 3,900-square-foot house located on a modest lot adjacent to a waterway in a suburban development on Longboat Key, Florida. Despite the relatively dense suburban setting, the clients desired openness and privacy.

Structural systems: Concrete block exterior walls; reinforced concrete floors and terraces; cast-in-place concrete and steel columns; wood and steel frame interior walls and roof structure.

Primary materials: Lime-based paint on water treated stucco for columns and block walls; concrete tile roof; stucco, marble, and drywall interior walls; stained concrete floors.

Mechanical systems: Gas-fired heating; forced air supply/central return air conditioner. House also relies on natural cross ventilation and covered porches to provide shade.

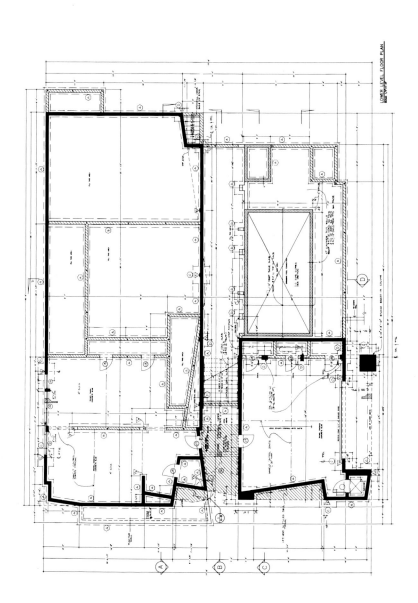

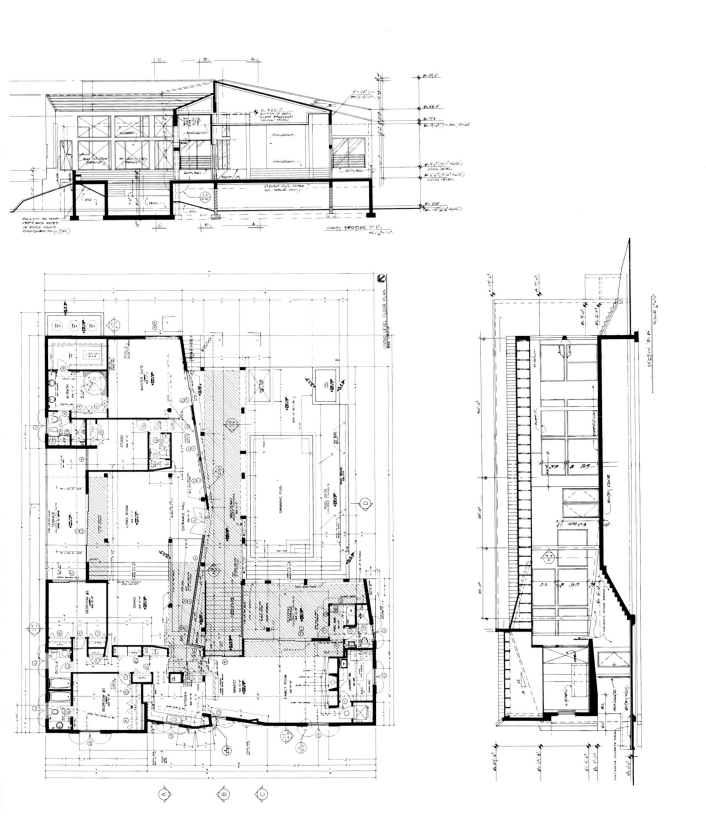

73

76

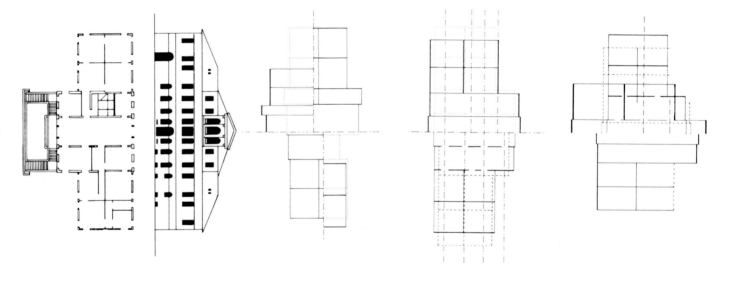

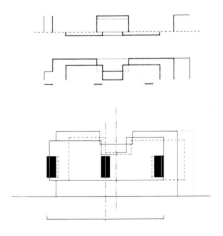

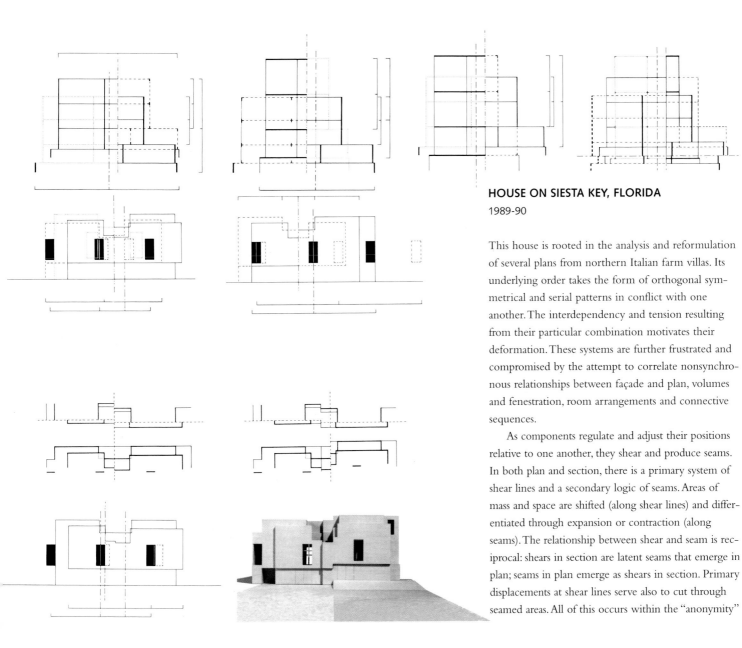

HOUSE ON SIESTA KEY, FLORIDA
1989-90

This house is rooted in the analysis and reformulation of several plans from northern Italian farm villas. Its underlying order takes the form of orthogonal symmetrical and serial patterns in conflict with one another. The interdependency and tension resulting from their particular combination motivates their deformation. These systems are further frustrated and compromised by the attempt to correlate nonsynchronous relationships between façade and plan, volumes and fenestration, room arrangements and connective sequences.

As components regulate and adjust their positions relative to one another, they shear and produce seams. In both plan and section, there is a primary system of shear lines and a secondary logic of seams. Areas of mass and space are shifted (along shear lines) and differentiated through expansion or contraction (along seams). The relationship between shear and seam is reciprocal: shears in section are latent seams that emerge in plan; seams in plan emerge as shears in section. Primary displacements at shear lines serve also to cut through seamed areas. All of this occurs within the "anonymity"

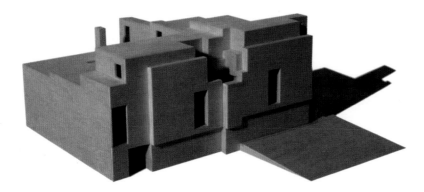

and material uniformity of the external shell. Thus the strategic shift from primary to secondary division treats heterogeneity as homogeneity and establishes conceptual tension through material coherence.

Conceptual determinants can be interpreted as material givens, or 'grounds' out of which programmatic elements are carved. In addition, the systems of order are affected by several requirements: the site, which is bounded by houses on both sides (by a street at the front and a waterway at the back); a local building ordinance that requires all living spaces to be elevated above a flood plane; and the clients, who have asked for privacy at the street and north side as well as openness toward views east of the site. Together, these requirements are accommodated behind a massive street facade, raised above garages, in which are embedded small, contiguous cellular spaces including, from the north: the master bathroom, guest bathroom, a small courtyard, laundry room, and a mechanical/storage room. Behind this zone, the main floor is divided into four areas organized from the north: master bedroom, dining and living rooms, kitchen, private entrance stair. These spaces take advantage of a breezeway, a covered porch, and a stepped corner terrace while the upstairs bedrooms share a roof terrace.

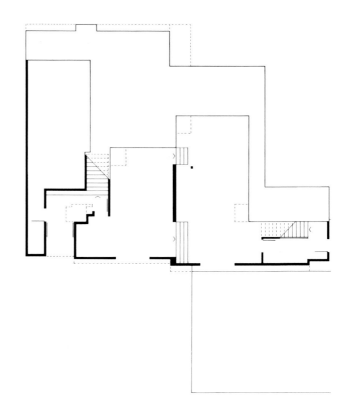

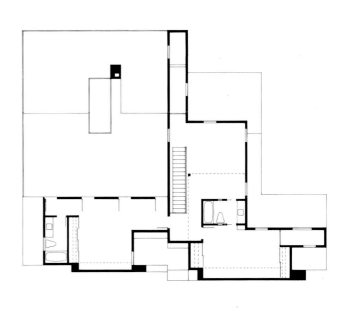

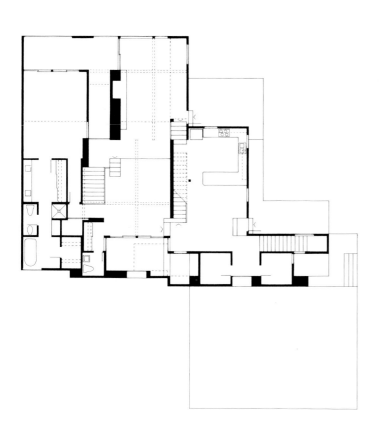

Program: 2,700-square-foot house for a couple with teenage children located in a development on Siesta Key, near Sarasota, Florida.

Structural systems: Concrete block and wood frame exterior and interior walls; reinforced concrete floors and terraces; cast-in-place concrete columns.

Primary materials: Integrally colored stucco exterior; gravel roof; marble, tile, and stained concrete floors, sidewalk, and driveway.

Mechanical systems: Gas-fired heating; forced air supply/central return air conditioner. The house also relies on cross breezes and shaded areas for cooling.

Beginning at the façade, entrances, sequences, and volumetric divisions establish two distinct living areas. At the north end, one sequence begins with the main entry/stair hall and garage, leads up to the living and dining rooms, and eventually to the main bedroom. At the south end, the ramp and raised garage, private entrance and stair lead to the kitchen from which a stair continues to the upper bedrooms. Programmatic volumes and familiar features such as fireplace, stairs, windows, floors, and ceilings are shaped from the aforementioned interlocking ordering systems. Connections provided by this complex formal syntax at the core force activities to the periphery of the house. The tension between opposing areas of emphasis effect the perception of arrangements commonly associated with the contemporary domestic program.

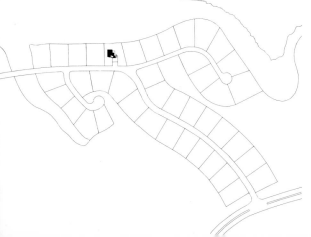

82

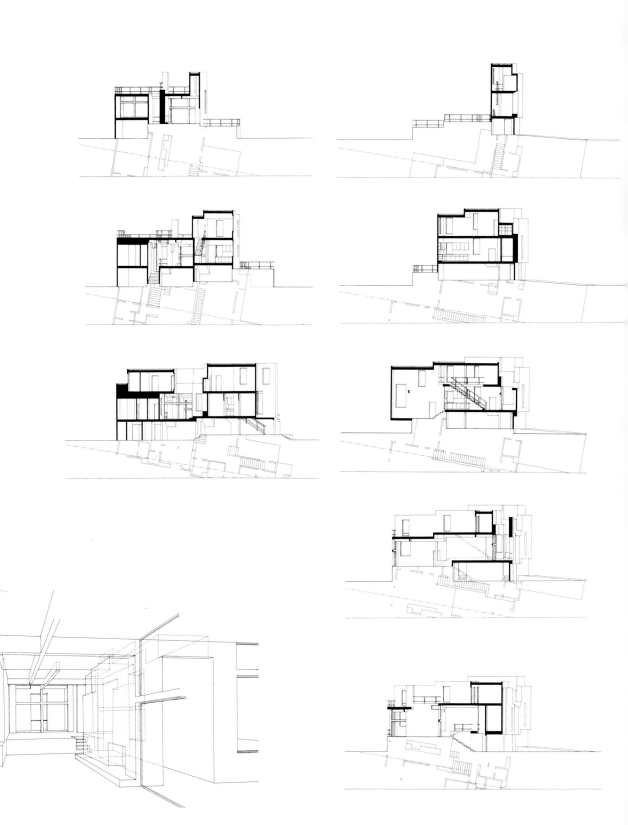

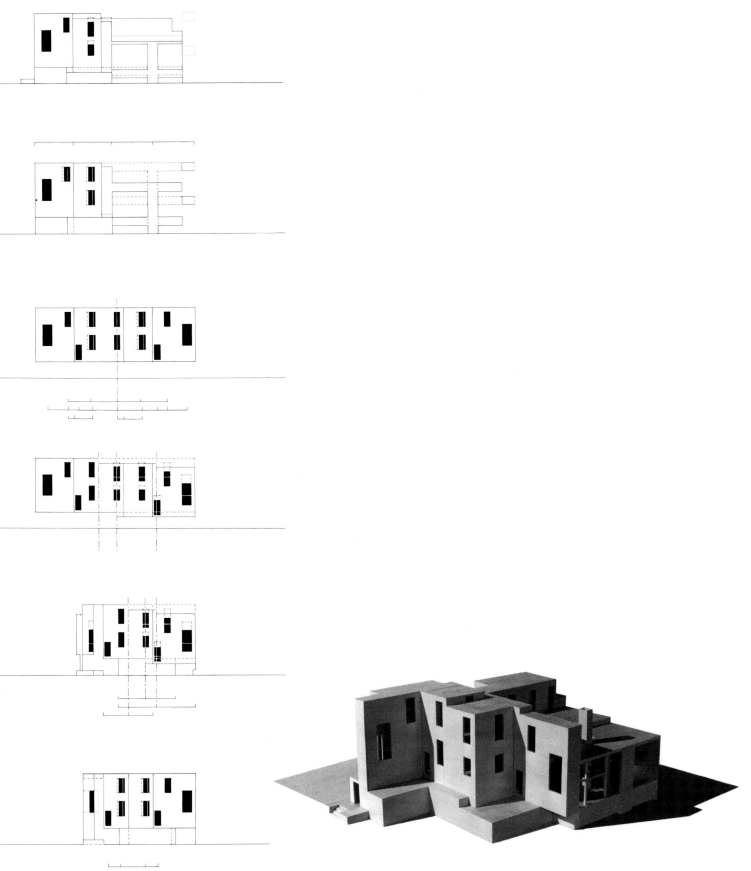

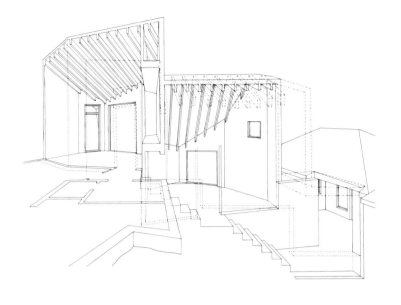

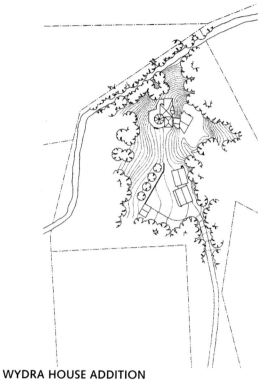

Existing House

WYDRA HOUSE ADDITION
Greendell, New Jersey
1987

This addition to the Wydra House doubles its size. The pre-existing house was primarily composed of additions to additions of volumes containing single spaces. Rather than imitating this accretive process, this addition uses the hill flanking the existing structures as the impetus to create a hybrid form. The addition can be understood as two contiguous volumes or as a continuous form sheared in order to step up the hill. In either case, the plan of the front edge of the addition seems to be a derivation of the existing octagonal living room. It suggests a subtractive process whereby an implicit original mass would have occupied a larger footprint. The gabled elevation on the uphill side reinforces this possibility by implying that it is the extruded end of a rather stout "wide load" suburban house.

The staircase in the addition converts an existing bedroom into a hall. This serves to suggest an interchangeability between the functions of rooms and passages that was already conceivable due to the contiguity of existing rooms.

Program: 1,100-square-foot addition for a blacksmith/jeweler.

Structural systems: Concrete block and wood frame exterior walls.

Primary materials: Standing seam metal roof; lime-based paint on water treated stucco; drywall interior walls and wood plank floors.

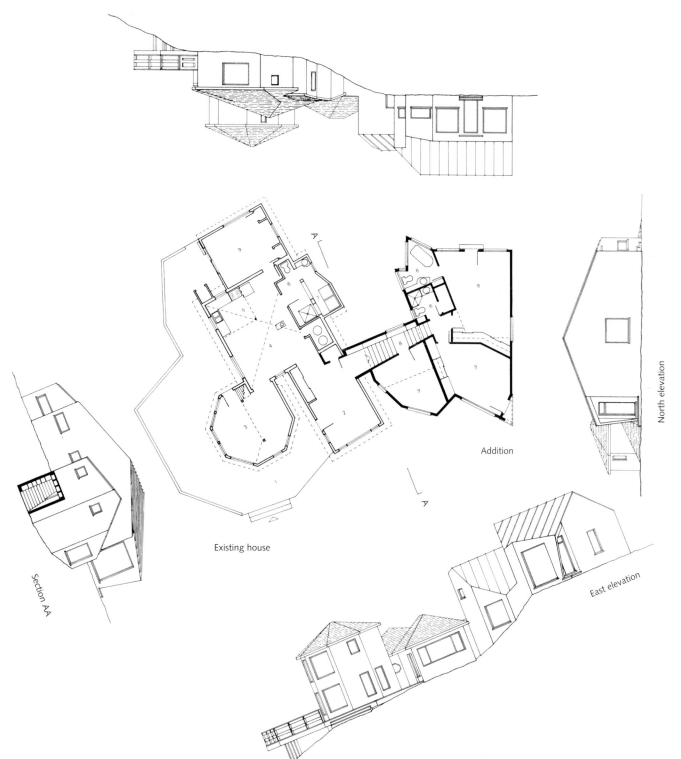

Section AA

Existing house

Addition

North elevation

East elevation

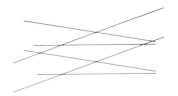
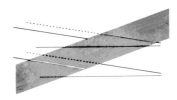

CORNERED HOUSE

Sarasota, Florida

1991–92

With this house, references to conventional suburban types become the afterimages of a series of crossing and parallel lines. The profile of an elongated and folded back frontal pediment coincides with the lines of a laterally disposed hip or gable ended roof. This combination is developed by way of three initial sets of parallel lines that have been bent, broken, and spliced, such that they are in the process of severing and displacing one another. In order to become interdependent, the lines turn now as pediment, now as fold, intersection, or edge—from form to meaning to form again.

The result is a dualism between outward appearances and latent geometries, between facts and implications: the bleached, suburban tectonic of the house subverts the logic of the lineaments that govern its formal make-up. This problem parallels that aspect of architecture and other arts whereby the medium through which a work is conceived is not the same as the medium through which it is realized.[1]

Overall, the house appears to be either three elongated volumes compressed into the same space or a

single, hollow vessel that folds in response to pressures from within. It is also reasonable to assume an additive process in which the central volume has been skewed and sheared in order to accommodate several appended faceted masses.

Whether the house is experienced as multiple or single, mass or surface, it suggests a reduction of spatial depth. From the street, the three implied volumes are rendered as several perspective or axonometric projections; the viewer is virtually situated at once above and in front of the house. This view collapses the house back into two dimensions and confounds its appearance as a voluminous object. The sense of flatness is reinforced by the termination of key segments of several profile lines between planes.

The house incorporates the morphology of neighborhood streets and the roof edges and ridges of nearby houses. But this incorporation is elusive. For example, if one is looking for a datum plane with which to refer the house to the site, there is some doubt about which walls are primary or fixed and which are secondary or skewed. The most forward wall plane inflects away from the adjacent street corner, breaks its orthogonal relationship to the other houses and the streets and thereby denies its status as a datum. As a result, the elongated volume embedded in the house

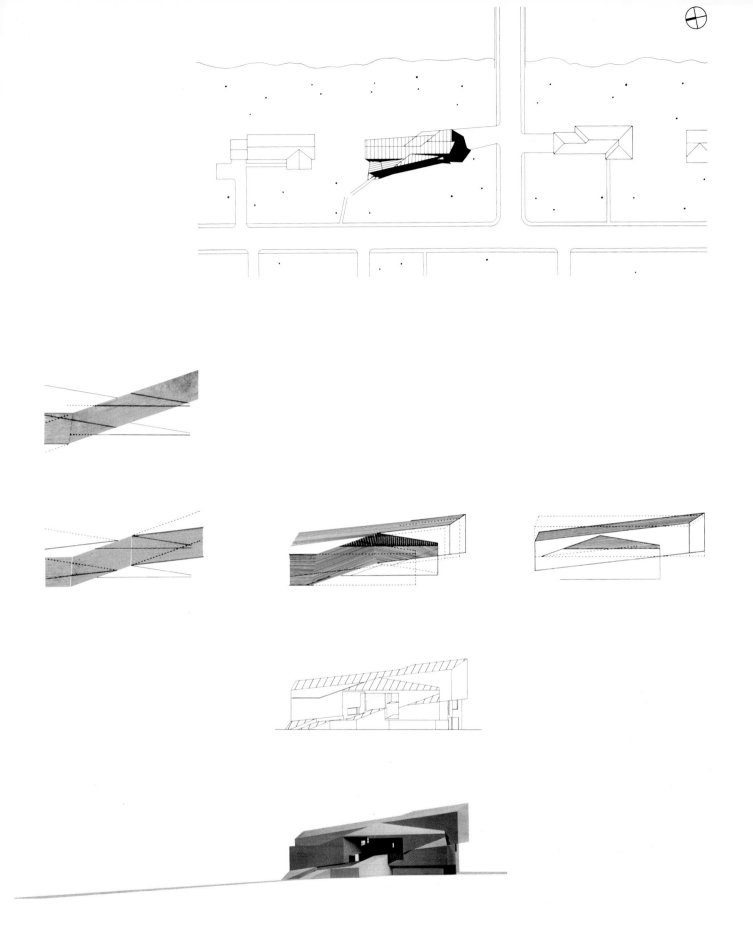

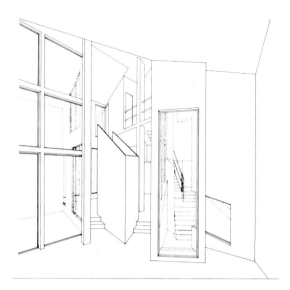

88

that appears skewed inside becomes orthogonal to the site; that is, the internal and external contextual logics exchange roles.

The interior is divided into roughly four irregular zones; looking from the front and beginning on the left, the first contains two bedrooms; the second, the den, kitchen, and back porch; the third, the front porch and dining room; and the fourth, the garage, living room, and upper bedroom. In the narrow space between the front and back porches the house appears to be bisected by a staircase into roughly two similar open areas.

The den, kitchen, dining, and living rooms are formed by two inverted and overlapping chevrons shifted off the center of the house. Residual gaps left over by the chevrons provide room for outdoor ter-races within the boundaries of the house.

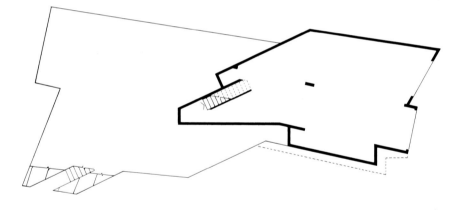

1. Architecture is allographic to the extent that the relationship between the drawing and the building, like the relationship of the score to performed music or the engraver's plate to the print, involves discrepancy. See Peter Kivy, *Sound and Semblance: Reflec-tions on Musical Representation* (Ithaca, NY: Cornell University Press, 1984), 85–107.

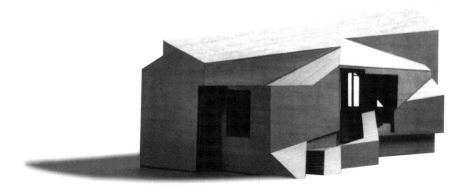

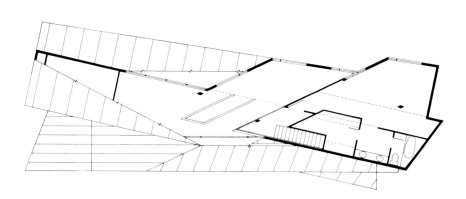

Program: 2,600-square-foot house located on a corner site adjacent to a waterway in Sarasota, Florida.

Structural systems: Concrete block and wood frame exterior and interior walls; reinforced concrete floors and terraces; cast-in-place concrete columns.

Primary materials: Integrally colored stucco; standing seam metal on roof and ramped surfaces; marble, tile, and stained concrete floors, sidewalk, and driveway.

Mechanical systems: Gas-fired heating; forced air supply/central return air conditioner. The house also relies on natural cross ventilation.

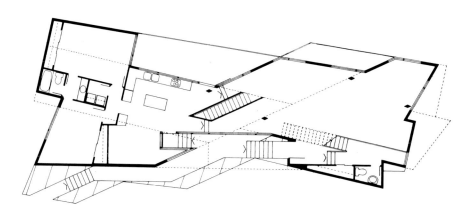

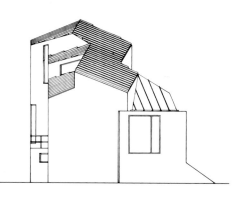

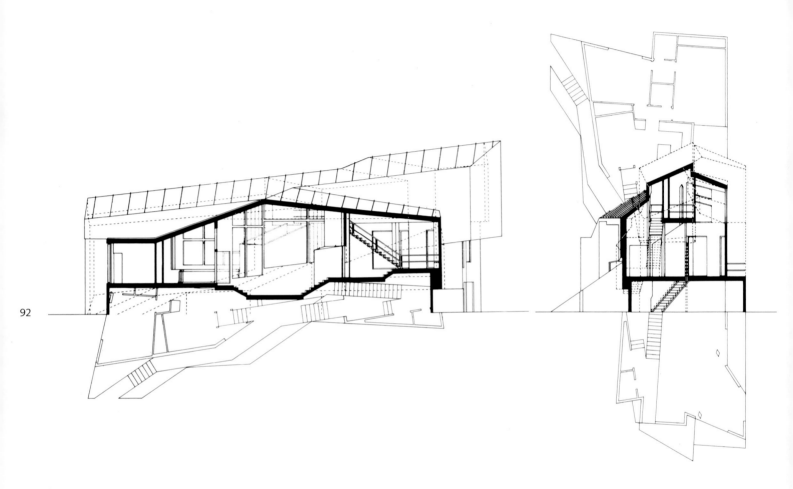

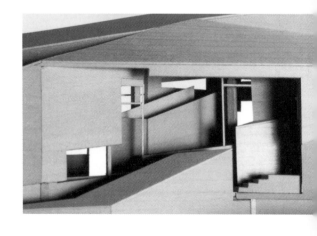

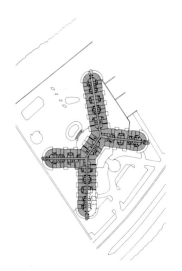

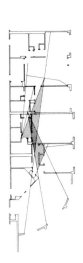

Muss Corridor
Miami Beach, 1994

This project offers a distinct alternative to the suggested plan for joining adjacent one- and two-bedroom units in an existing Miami Beach apartment building. Except for the introduction of an interior window, this project deploys unexceptional details and remains within the constraints of the standard low cost materials and building techniques provided by the in-house construction staff.

Normally, these two unit types would be connected by a long, narrow, shifting, orthogonal corridor that separates the existing bedrooms from their previously adjacent service spaces (bathrooms, dressing rooms, and closets). This standard solution is interrupted by vertical structure and mechanical shafts that do not align from one unit to the other. In this project, a series of skewed walls connect the irregularly disposed fixed elements. In the meantime, the exceptional shape of the new corridor subsumes the previously exceptional kitchen and disguises the awkward problem of having a line of bathrooms on the opposite side of the corridor from the bedrooms. For example, the main bedroom—formerly an L–shaped living /dining room—is linked to two separate bathrooms.

Three niches punctuate the corridor; one remains empty and two serve to consolidate irregular groups of doors. In these areas, routine parallel walls bend in such a way that familiar doors and frames become partially hidden from within the rooms.

A soffit in the living room connects the corner window of the library with a corner opening into the corridor. Approaching the two similarly folded yet oppositely open corners, the window appears to be part of a prismatic solid. By association, other folded walls can be interpreted as fragments of a transitory membrane between incomplete volumes and masses.

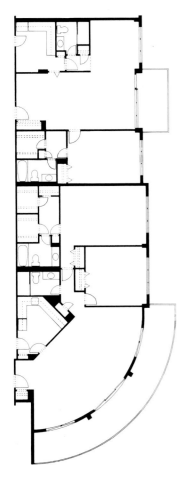
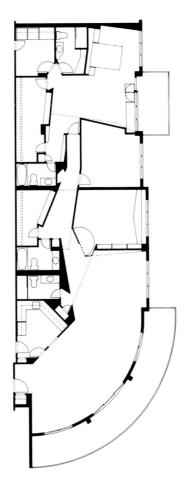

Existing Plan showing two separate units.

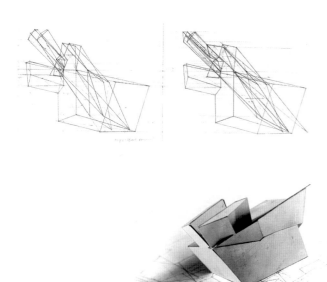

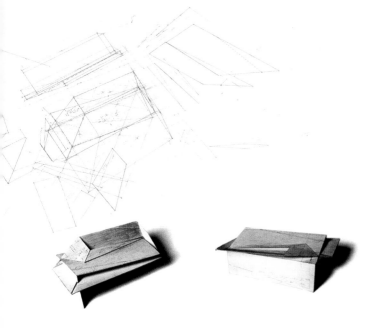

Stilicho I
1993
Variations on a perspective projected in elevation as a stereotomic object.

96

Presso Villa Marco I
1993
A vernacular, orthogonal block is mirrored, distorted and intersected by a perspectival/stereotomic object serving as its roof. The roof is an inverted, horizontally attenuated recapitulation of the primary block to which it is systematically related by means of a Taylorian Perspective.

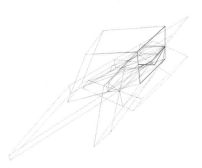

STEREOTOMIC PERMUTATIONS
1993–98

In his 1929 Barcelona Pavilion, Ludwig Mies van der Rohe rotated architecture's traditional vertical axis of bilateral symmetry into the horizon of vision.[1] Symmetry, no longer bound to the ideal human body, instead began to codify of the phenomenon of reflection. But there is a notable difference between Mies's reflections and those found on water along the horizon. By imparting equal dimensions, angles, and proportions to things above and below a horizontal axis, Mies's symmetry implied that reflection was not susceptible to contingencies of perception.

Reflection is an unlikely configuration in architecture, particularly when it is unrelated to the horizon. Although dualistic symmetry (as in reflection, without a central figure) permeates architecture in all of its scales, its properties of replication and inversion are invariant; it lacks the distortion characteristic of the experience of reflection.

In Stereotomic Permutations, the inequivalencies of reflective symmetry are given a form. Symmetry with inequality can be found in the conjunction of two distinct, though related, projection techniques: stereotomy and distance point perspective. Stereotomy,

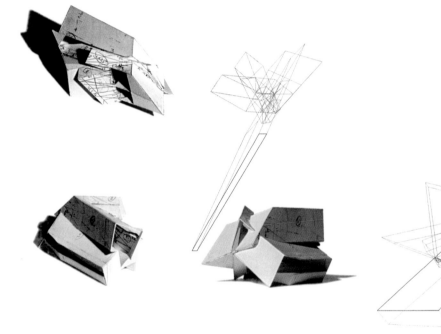

House with a Carport in the Attic
Underneath
1994

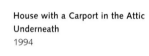

Presso Villa Marco III
1994

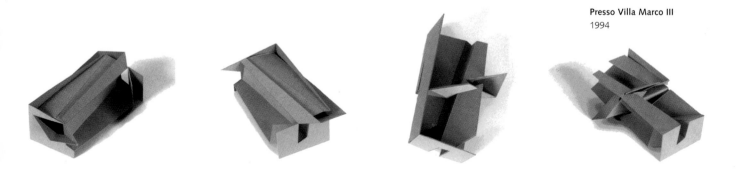

an orthographic method of projection used to direct the cutting of stone, involves convergence, a property it shares with perspective and sciagraphy (shadow projection). This likeness between methods allows them to be combined. Thus, it is possible for a perspective or a shadow drawn on a plane surface to be inflated into a full-bodied volume as though it had been cut from stone.

The two-point Taylorian perspective apparatus not only produces mirrored, non-identical twin forms, but it also creates sciagraphic projections linking objects to their shadows serially, through instances of coplanarity. The implication is twofold: on the one hand, we can imagine the deformation of symmetry and seriality as the elastic transformation of the proportions of one part of a dual object relative to the other. On the other hand, it suggests that the deformation is an effect of anamorphosis. In other words, it would appear that the distortion is actually a view—albeit a distorted one—of a symmetrical building rather than a perpendicular (frontal) view of a distorted building.

Anamorphosis is a perspective in which the central ray is sharply oblique rather than perpendicular to the picture plane. The frontal view thus presents distortions usually perceived only in the margins of con-

ventional perspectives. Anamorphosis superimposes obliquity onto frontality. In painting, anamorphosis requires that the spectator relocate to a peculiarly nonfrontal position in order to obtain an undistorted view of a figure. While moving from the frontal view to a specified marginal vantage point, the spectator witnesses a transformation of the figures depicted in the painting. In this sence, anamorphosis behaves as though it were a technique of architecture; it co-opts three-dimensional space and momentarily choreographs its inhabitation.

In "Stereotomic Permutations," perception causes distortion. Absolute symmetry or seriality thus become systems for obtaining undistorted views. As in anamorphic painting, attenuation and compression accelerate or slow the effect of diminution and magnification as though a volume had not yet been viewed from the very peculiar position from which it would achieve symmetry. In these projects, however, the Taylorian device and its combination with stereotomy do not offer a point from which the distortion would be "corrected." In that sense, they do not present cases of architecture imitating anamorphic painting— i.e., this architecture does not imitate a genre of painting that arguably imitates architecture. The anticipa-

Rectilinear Spiriculate
1998

tion of symmetry and seriality is met with the realization that the apparent anamorphosis is dysfunctional,
and thus remains an unfulfilled expectation. Finally,
anamorphosis itself becomes an unrealized reference.

   With its regular intervals, the grid has provided
the most legible bond between perspectival vision
and the built domain of architecture. Mies recast that
coalition by using the horizon of an idealized reflection as the term of connection. These projects propose
stereotomy as a new interlocutor between perspective
and three-dimensional, orthographic architectural
space. At the same time, symmetry and seriality appear
to be distorted by anamorphosis or the vicissitudes of
reflection.

1. Robin Evans, "Mies van der Rohe's Paradoxical Symmetries,"
   AA Files 19 (1990).

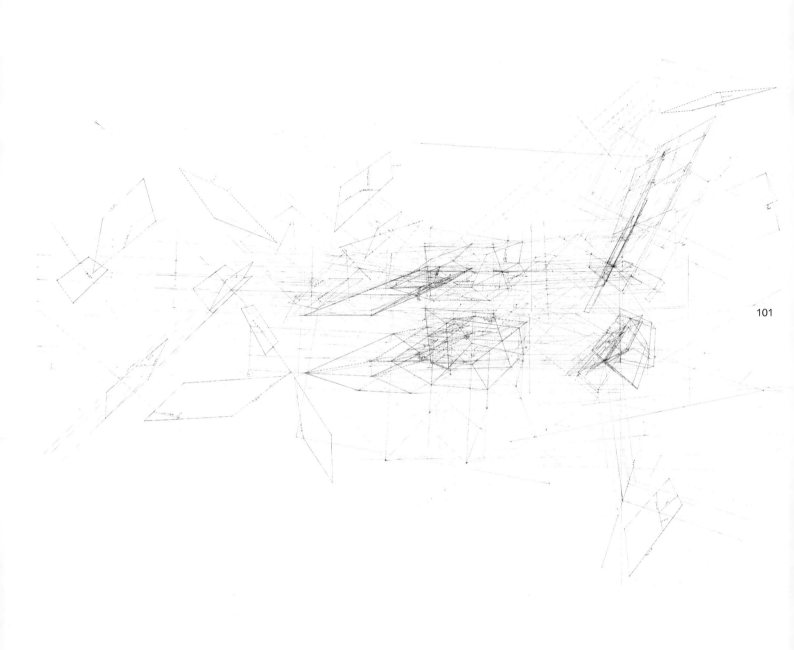

101

Presso Villa Marco III
The horizontally attenuated building hovers over its sloped site.
The roof/roof terrace, the sills of two similar windows, and stairs
(all generated by hybrid Boolean operations), are integrated into
a common building block. A driveway loops under and around a
voided chevron that provides passage to the first level terrace
and central entry.

102

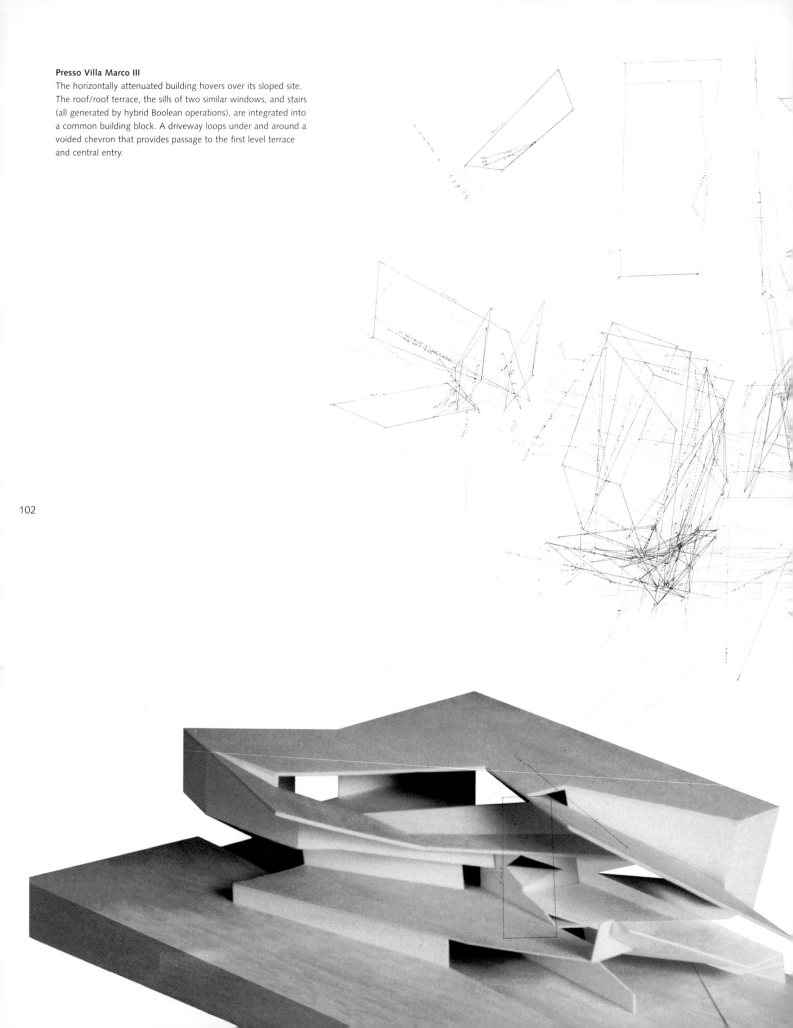

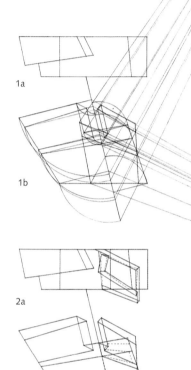

STILICHO DUPLEX
1994

The Taylorian perspective apparatus is capable of
reversing the roles of its objects and perspectives relative to one another. Planes and lines of coincidence
provide links between various volumetric permutations. All of the surfaces of the building, their true
shapes, intersections, joining details, and lines of convergence, collapse four spatial types: "ground" (the
original object); "void" (based on a perspective of a
two-dimensional plane); planes (based on a perspective of a three-dimensional volume); and "solid" (based
on a perspective of "void"). Inside and outside, back
and front, beginning and end, plane, volume, mass and
void appear simultaneously.

Projective systems convert each arbitrarily introduced iteration into a necessity. Once instantiated,
each constituent is systematically linked by its configuration, dimension, and proportion to aggregations
previous as well as forthcoming. As if modeled on
Leibniz's monadology, the axis of each verifiable distortion redefines the whole with respect to its parts.
Furthermore, the axes are diffused or partially hidden
by the uninterrupted surfaces and consequential

1a

1b

2a

2b

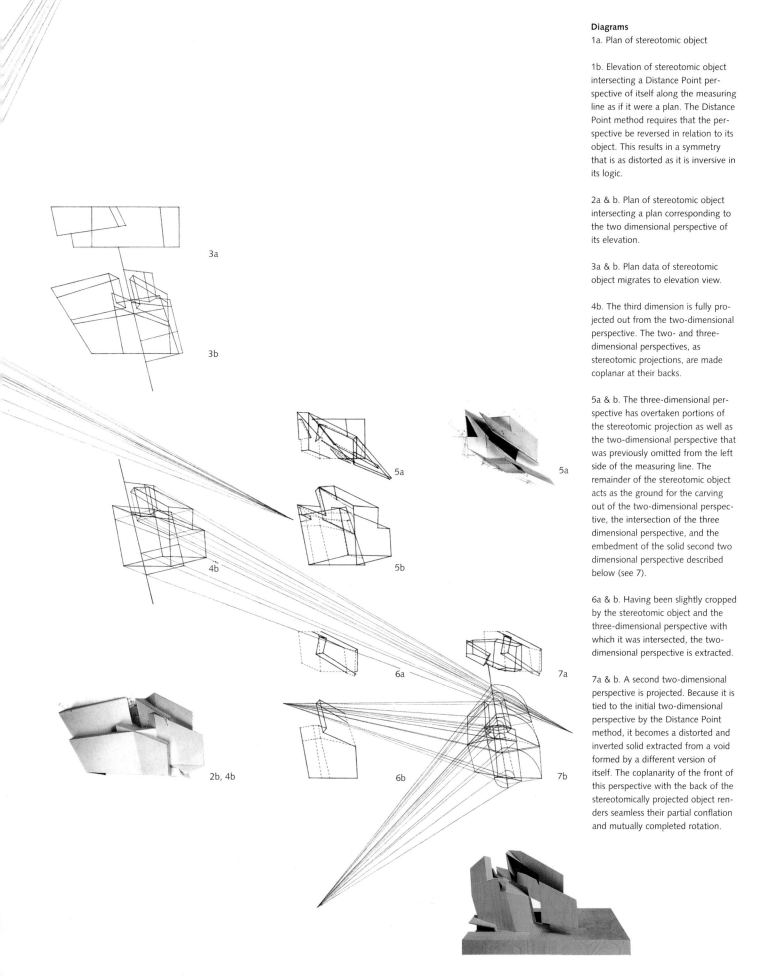

Diagrams

1a. Plan of stereotomic object

1b. Elevation of stereotomic object intersecting a Distance Point perspective of itself along the measuring line as if it were a plan. The Distance Point method requires that the perspective be reversed in relation to its object. This results in a symmetry that is as distorted as it is inversive in its logic.

2a & b. Plan of stereotomic object intersecting a plan corresponding to the two dimensional perspective of its elevation.

3a & b. Plan data of stereotomic object migrates to elevation view.

4b. The third dimension is fully projected out from the two-dimensional perspective. The two- and three-dimensional perspectives, as stereotomic projections, are made coplanar at their backs.

5a & b. The three-dimensional perspective has overtaken portions of the stereotomic projection as well as the two-dimensional perspective that was previously omitted from the left side of the measuring line. The remainder of the stereotomic object acts as the ground for the carving out of the two-dimensional perspective, the intersection of the three dimensional perspective, and the embedment of the solid second two dimensional perspective described below (see 7).

6a & b. Having been slightly cropped by the stereotomic object and the three-dimensional perspective with which it was intersected, the two-dimensional perspective is extracted.

7a & b. A second two-dimensional perspective is projected. Because it is tied to the initial two-dimensional perspective by the Distance Point method, it becomes a distorted and inverted solid extracted from a void formed by a different version of itself. The coplanarity of the front of this perspective with the back of the stereotomically projected object renders seamless their partial conflation and mutually completed rotation.

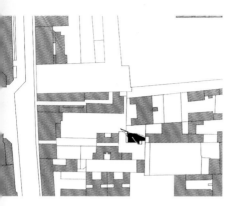

intersections of their three-dimensionality. Inextricably linked and always potentially determinative, the axes register different portions of objects and perspectives with reference to different orientations, degrees of concealment and interference between them. The axes become the intervals of a variegated series.

This project is as integral to the inside of this block in the Twentieth Arrondissement of Paris as it is to the systems of projection by which it was determined. Replacing two small houses (already demolished), it engages existing yard walls and passageways in a manner that alters the relationship between public and private spaces of surrounding buildings. While its primary orthogonal volume is continuous with the morphology of the block, other facets of its inflected form transgress pre-established boundaries. On the one hand the duplex avoids crowding its neighbors by shrinking from them; on the other hand, its attenuated components, resting or leaning on existing walls, imply connections between diagonally opposite spaces.

The two units are interlocked around stacked and staggered staircases along a wall that bifurcates the interior. An exterior stair penetrates the building and provides entry into unit 1 while stairs in unit 2 navigate left over interstices. Unit 2 gains access to a

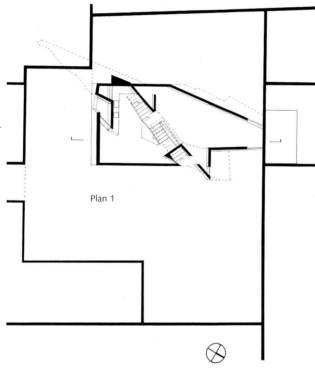

Plan 1

walled garden at ground level; unit 1 benefits from a covered roof terrace created by a negative volume based on the two dimensional perspective from which it was projected.

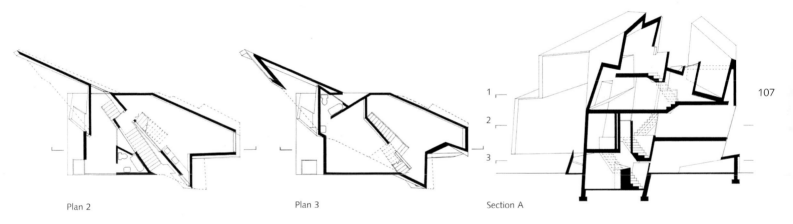

Plan 2   Plan 3   Section A

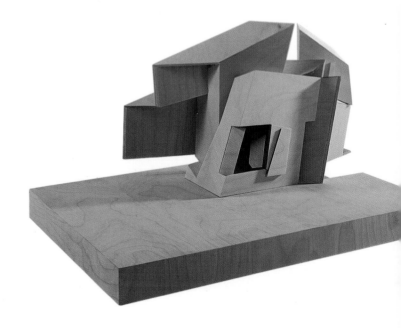

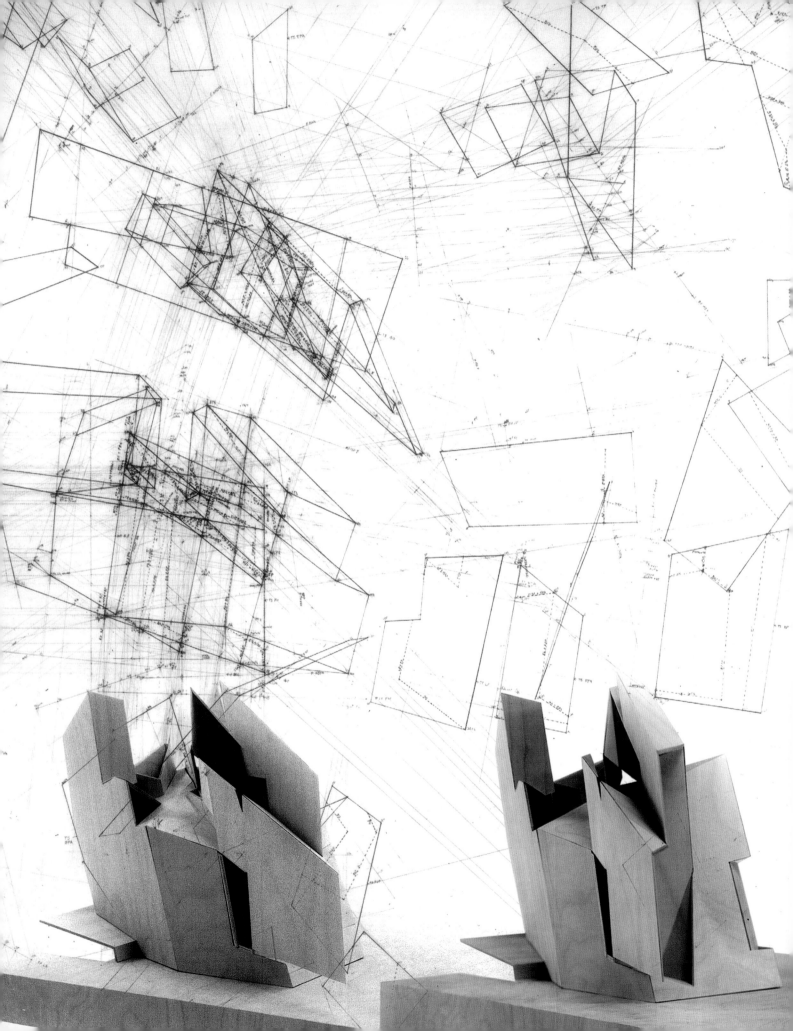

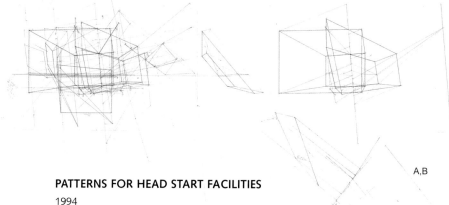

A,B

PATTERNS FOR HEAD START FACILITIES
1994

This competition proposal for a Head Start community and educational facility is composed of variously scaled and attenuated versions of a single volumetric object. Transformed by perspectival projection, programmatic volumes for adults and children, gathering and play, are drawn into successive permutations that remain in constant and discernible relation to each other. The process of projection is reversible; perspectives may serve as objects and vice versa. While these principles of derivation remain constant and repeatable, the variables intrinsic to them impart a logical flexibility. The method suggests a pattern in which each permutation can be informed by the particular circumstances of use and context.

The building challenges familiar distinction between two and three dimensions, and between surface, volume, and mass. The pattern of colored concrete shingles fluctuates between square and diamond depending upon the angle of the surface and the point from which it is observed. Its components are neither sufficiently large to read as figures nor sufficiently complete or repeated to become elements of a consistent texture. The bulk of the building seems

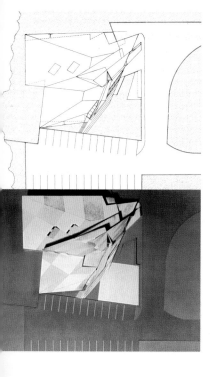

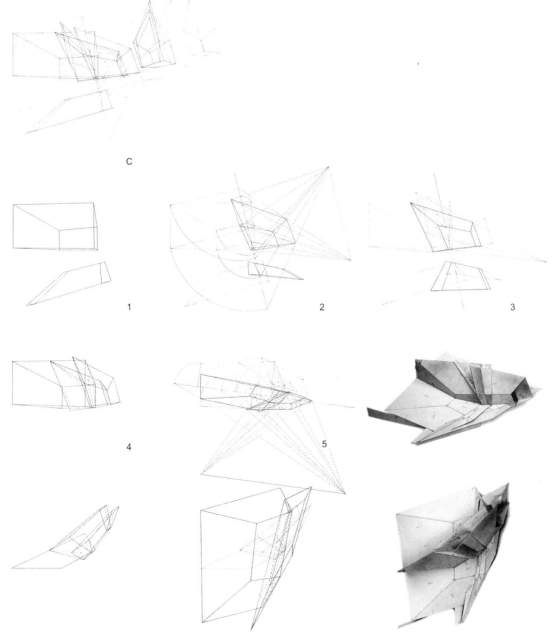

Diagrams

A,B,C: An initial perspective of a six sided object is assumed to be an orthographic projection (an elevation) from which other views (a section and a plan) are later derived to produce a third dimension. Preliminary variations of secondary perspectives establish a working schema for deformation of symmetry along a near vertical axis.

1. Elevation and plan of volume containing the adult and community services.

2. Elevation and plan of adult and community volume intersecting a perspective of itself along a measuring line. The resulting horizontally attenuated volumes house the educational facilities.

3. Plan data is calibrated with the elevation along the measuring line. The third dimension is fully projected into perspective to form the multipurpose room.

4. Gathering space and multipurpose room are joined and intersected to create space for the entry, kitchen, terrace, and mezzanine.

5. A second perspective is taken of the earlier object combined with its perspective as though they were one entity. The broader of the resulting horizontal volumes houses the classrooms and community programs. The narrowest, most attenuated portion contains service spaces; its compression provides space for the playground out front.

C

1

2

3

4

5

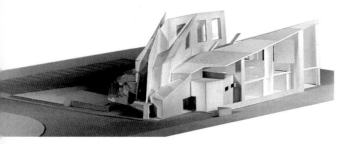

112

stretched and flattened in order to face both the street and the adjacent parking lot at once; its withdrawal from both, marked by bleachers, provides a foreground for the play area and immediate access to the heart of the building. As a result, the playground gains a position of prominence contiguous to key interior programs.

The configuration of the building provides various opportunities for children to gauge their relative size. The vertically attenuated volume contains adult and community services and the horizontally attenuated space covers the educational facilities. An interactive spatial link is situated at the point where the initial programmatic volumes (for adults and for children, gathering and play—all subtle permutations of one another) intersect to form shared gathering areas (entry, kitchen, multipurpose room, mezzanine, terraces, and playground). Within the complex interstices of the intersections exist the most fluid spaces. Staff conference/observation rooms hover above and straddle the classrooms. The terrace beside the play area links with the upper multipurpose room and extends into the mezzanine level, which rests on the edge of the kitchen below. Views are shared between the upper story and each of the classrooms below. Balconies and joined common areas are illuminated by clerestory and strategically isolated windows.

Section B

Section C

114

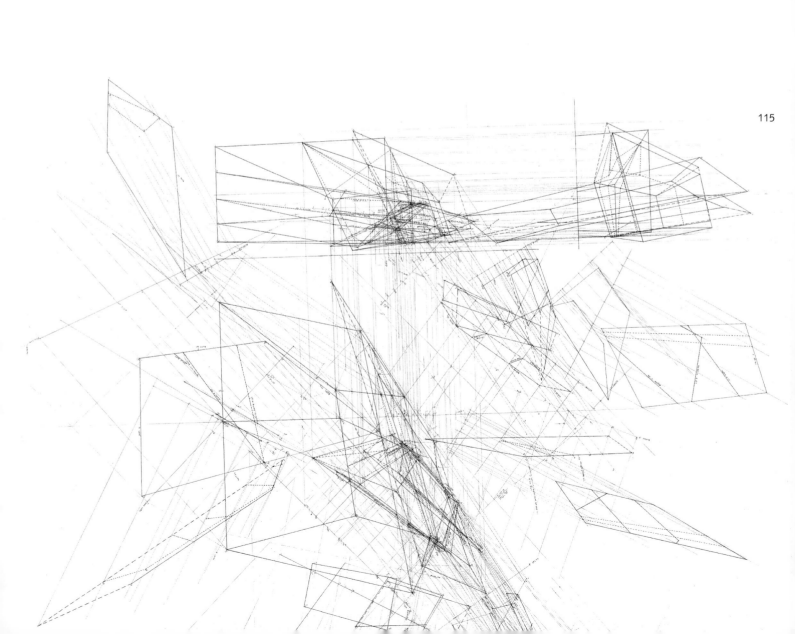

Section A

Section D

116

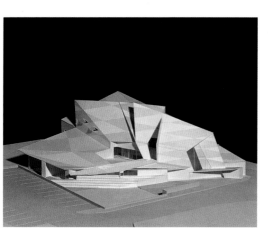
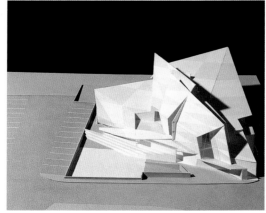

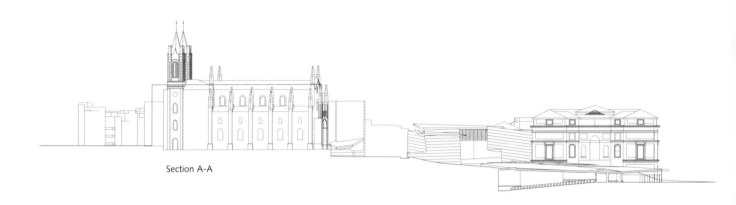

Section A-A

COMPETITION PROPOSAL FOR THE EXPANSION OF THE MUSEO DEL PRADO

Madrid, Spain
1996

This proposal for an addition to the Prado both flanks and foregrounds the museum's eighteenth-century Juan de Villanueva Building (fig 5.1) The simultaneous affirmation and denial of frontality, symmetry, verticality, and solidity reflects the equivocal imperatives posed by the competition program: to leave the Villanueva Building virtually unscathed, to keep a low profile, and to become a subsidiary annex while creating a new entrance, with all of its attendant implications of primacy.

The program for the addition calls for relieving the Prado from crowding caused by contemporary museum services. Additional public facilities including a new ticketing and coat check area, temporary galleries, an auditorium, and service and administrative function spaces would allow the museum to recover gallery areas within the Villanueva Building that are presently consumed by these functions.

This project proposes an addition that is neither an appendage nor a device for unifying disparate urban elements, but rather a simultaneously coherent and

inflected form, complete unto itself. The form of the main part of the proposal is derived from a volume of circuitous lineaments related to the north façade of the Villanueva Building (presently the main entrance to the museum). Coinciding perspectival and stereotomic projections produce what would appear to be a three-dimensional anamorphoses. Yet, as a consequence of the projective techniques employed, the position from which the anamorphosis would be fully encompassed can never be occupied. Such is the trajectory of vision, as opposed to the fixity of sight, which the fusion of stereotomy and perspective entails.

Proposal

The proposal consists of two closely related parts. The first, an entrance building and plaza, would reshape the experience of entering the Prado into an extended urban and architectural event by means of a portico that folds into a plinth on the plaza. The second, an extended stair in the San Jeronimos cloister and a new building bounding the cloister, would house the library, archives, and administrative functions of the museum. Significantly, the form of the cloister intervention—its plinth would join with a new building, which in turn bounds the cloister—rhymes with the spiral sequence of the entrance building, conceptually

linking the two parts of the proposal.

The proposed entrance building is located behind the Villanueva Building and flanks its north façade (fig 5.2). Given its size and proximity to the tour entry-point in the Villanueva Building, this site offers the most opportune location for a new entrance façade that can replace the original monumental entrance with one that is comparably significant. The existing secondary entrance at the center of the long front of the Villanueva Building would serve as a ceremonial entrance for special events. In this way, the proposal recognizes the history of the linear sequence of the Prado that, for the most part, has proceeded from one end to the other rather than centrifugally from the central portico.

The plaza is bound by the new and old façades of the Prado on one side and the Hotel Ritz Savoy on the other (fig 5.3). Holding an edge, the museum will participate in the definition of a significant urban space—critical, given that the Villanueva Building, already an object, is susceptible to disengagement because it can no longer provide for its own entrance functions. To prevent the Real Academia Espanola, at the top of this new plaza, from diverting too much symbolic attention from the Prado, the façade of the new entrance building subtly inflects toward the Plaza

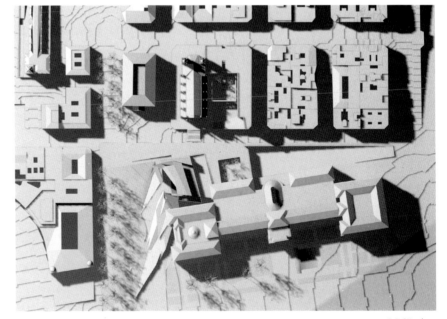

5.3 Siteplan.

5.5

del Castillo placing the Academia in deeper background. The new plinth replaces the existing stair (fig
5.4) and conceals the Villanueva Building's relationship
to the ground (fig 5.5). In a sense, it restores the condition that existed before the twentieth century, when
the ground rose directly to the museum's second level
(figs 5.6 & 5.7). It also recollects an earlier staircase
(fig 5.8) later replaced by the current condition.

Perspective and Stereotomy

The project addresses the particular problems posed by
the requirements of the addition throuhg the wider
thematic of a formal method. The addition expands,
contracts, mirrors, multiplies, and distorts according to
perspectival projections as they coincide with
stereotomy. The result is an inner shaping of form
through inflection of distance point perspective, a projection technique that binds its objects and perspectives by reversing them along a shared axis; stereotomy
transforms these into three-dimensional volumes
which apparently creates a volatile kind of symmetry.

The consequence of this distortion is a certain
anamorphic effect caused by the expectation of familiar symmetry; such is the trajectory of vision, as
opposed to the fixity of sight, which the fusion of
stereotomy and distance point perspective entails.

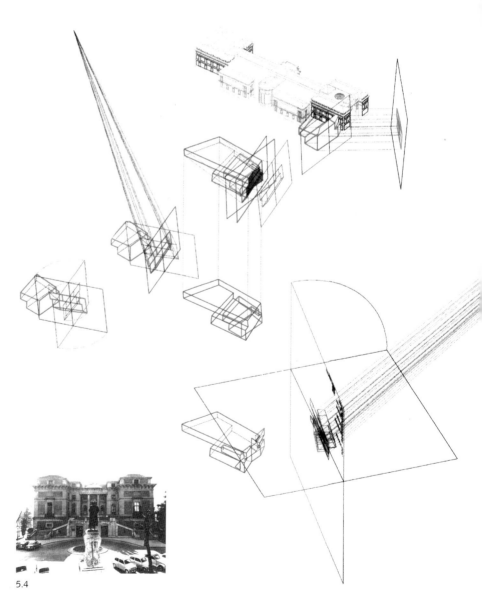

5.4

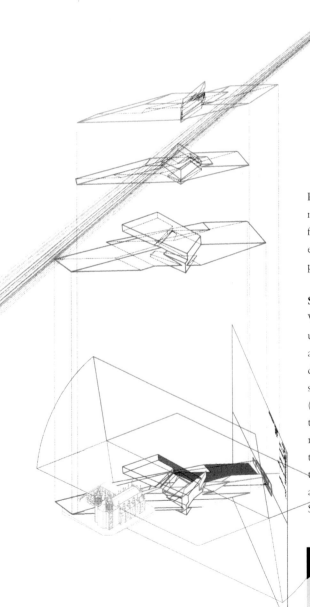

Perception and description, two tasks that are normally distinct in architecture, are thus subsumed under formal unity. Elasticity is implied by compression and expansion. Hence, stereotomy fused with the distance point method actuates a logic of coherence.

Sequence

Visitors are drawn into the new entrance by an attenuated plinth, which leads into a columnless portico and lobby. From there, the visitor has three options: descend to the south corner (toward the cafe, bookstore, and new galleries); descend to the north lobby (toward new galleries, an auditorium, and, ultimately, the ground floor of the Villanueva Building); ascend a ramp toward the old Prado and a view of the portico through which one has just entered. This last alternative defines the project: it allows the public to pursue a path that corresponds to the spiral meander of the San Jeronimos intervention.

5.6

5.7

5.8

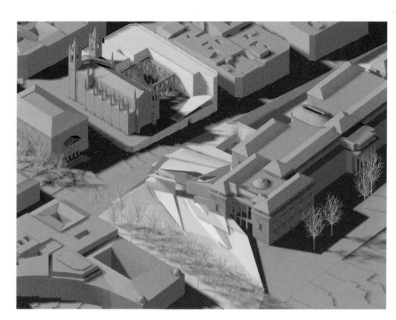

122

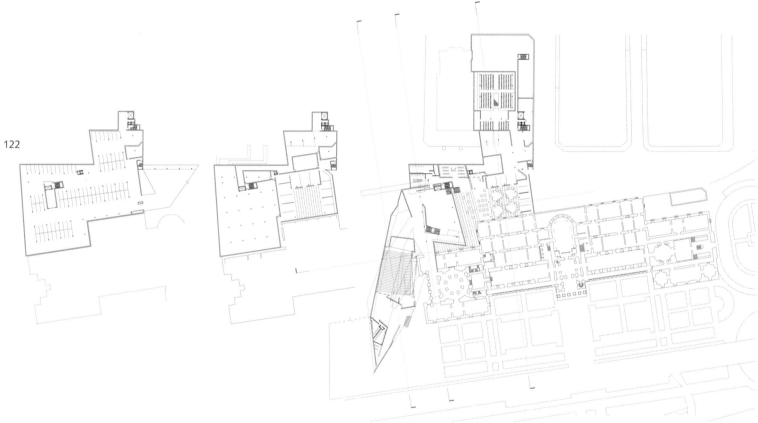

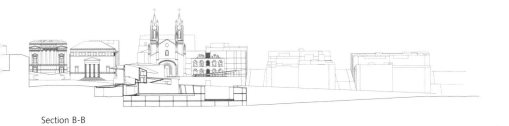

Section B-B

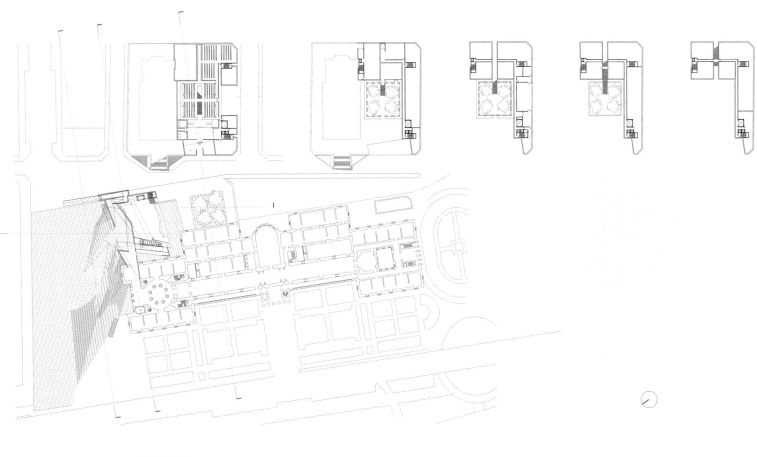

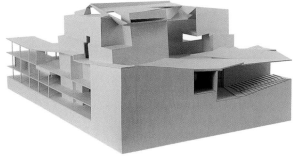

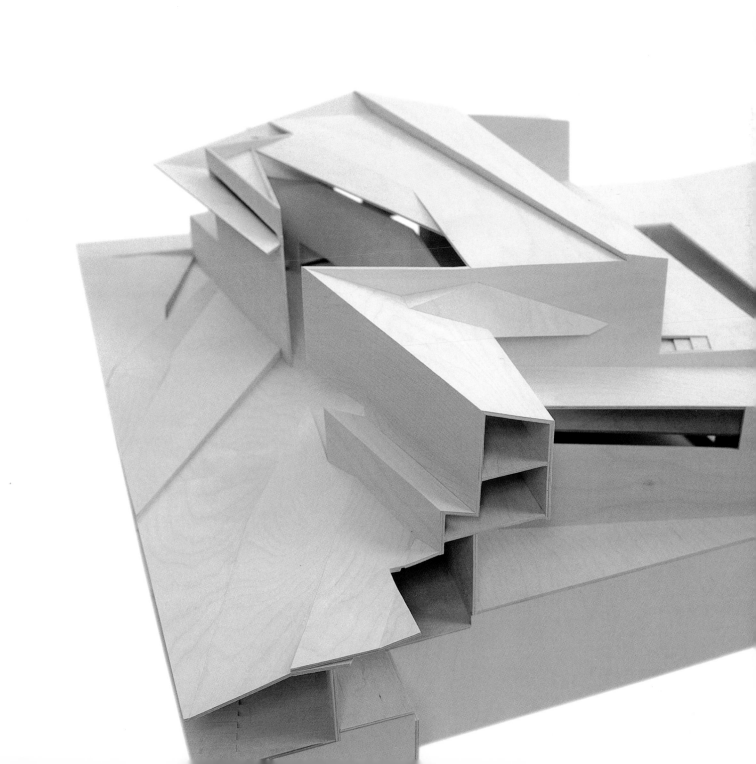

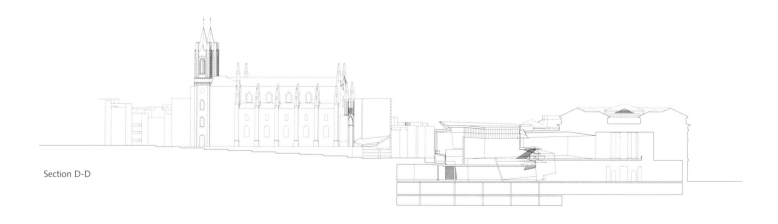

Section D-D

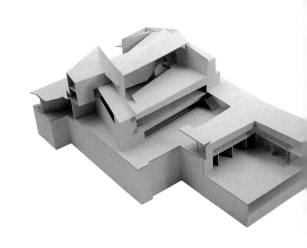

Tectonics of the Interior

The lower levels of the building are organized according to conventional column-and-slab construction that establishes a syntax independent from that of the stereotomic volumes above (A). Three columns from this subterranean area extend up to what will be three of the four most important beams in the upper areas of the stereotomic precinct (B). All of the columns terminate at the first (stereotomically defined) surface with which they intersect (C). While two extend to near equal height terminating at the top of the lobby, one is discontinued at the significantly lower mezzanine level.

From certain positions, the length of this particular column, apparently caused by its intersection with the mezzanine, correlates with the length of hidden or revealed portions of the taller pair. Thus, the hidden and truncated columns share a third system. This system would appear to be simultaneously bound to the stereotomic forms and the repositioning of the inhabitant that is immanent to the anamorphic effect.

By means of secondary beams, loads are transferred from the short column under the mezzanine to a series of three thinner columns that, in turn, support a fourth beam (C). Another pattern emerges upon close inspection of the short column; it seems to be "hammered down," truncated, and/or discontinued and replaced by the three thinner columns, which resume where it leaves off (D). According to similitude of number and interval in a straight line, the three thin columns provide a legible reference for the three wide columns that are idiosyncratic in height and distribution. Equal in number, the two sets may be perceived as derivatives of one another.

The three wide columns could arguably be understood as responding to the structural requirements of the stereotomic forms. However, rather than constructing a discrete system by themselves, the columns separately define different centrifugal spaces. Moreover, the columns independently imply spatial inflection, congestion, and compression relative to the spaces of the stereotomic forms that they foreground, divide, and support respectively. Effect and cause, the supported and its support, the after and before of tectonics, would appear to be interchangeable, to flicker between stereotomic and columnar formal systems.

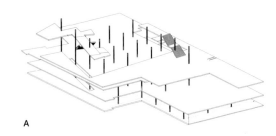

A

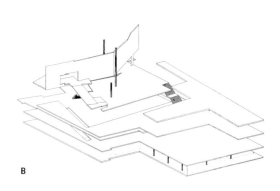

B

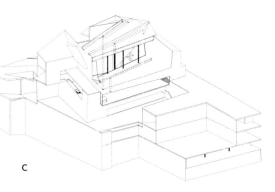

C

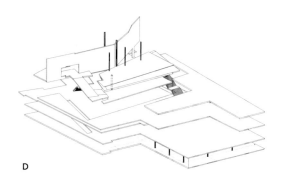

D

127

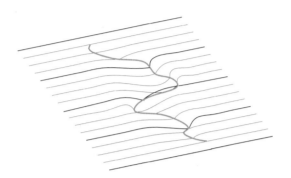

TERMINAL LINES
1998

Terminal line is a neologism used to describe a line entirely contained within the boundaries of a surface (fig. 1). What distinguishes a terminal line from all other lines is that it dissolves at its endpoints by becoming tangent with the very surface that generates it. The line coincides with the collection of points on the surface at which the rate of change of slope is discontinuous. In mathematics, this rate corresponds to the second derivative.

Though a terminal line can be brought about by tangency with a number of surface geometries, if it happens to dissolve into the flat surface then it is fused with a norm of contemporary buildings. A conventional manifestation of orthogonal construction, the flat surface, is made part of a particular instance of another geometry, topology. This synthesis represents a reversal of the tendency of contemporary architects to cull forms from outside architecture in order to make distinctive buildings. With the terminal line, a manifestation of orthogonal construction is co-opted by a geometry with which the quotidian usually remains largely incompatible.

In Montague House and Torus House, ordinary flat surfaces and the terminal line are reciprocally adaptive. Not only could the everyday condition of orthogonality be restored, if it were not for the disruption of the terminal line, but the terminal line could itself achieve a less awkwardly sinuous state, or even straighten out completely, if it were not confined to such specific orthogonal environments.

If the terminal line crosses a flat surface (wall, floor, and ceiling) for example, it treats them as if they were one. The straight lines between the conventional surfaces break along and curve to the terminal line and in so doing appear to be folds in a single surface rather than orthogonal intersections between several. To the extent that these lines seem themselves to be breaks in a continuous surface, they share properties of the terminal line while remaining distinct from it. Such a hybrid, incorporating characteristics of both the terminal line and lines between flat surfaces, portrays the former as being a part of the orthogonal system as opposed to an adaptation to it. The terminal line is nevertheless able to distinguish itself as an exception and intensify the very conditions in architecture that straight lines ordinarily maintain: flatness and orthogonality.

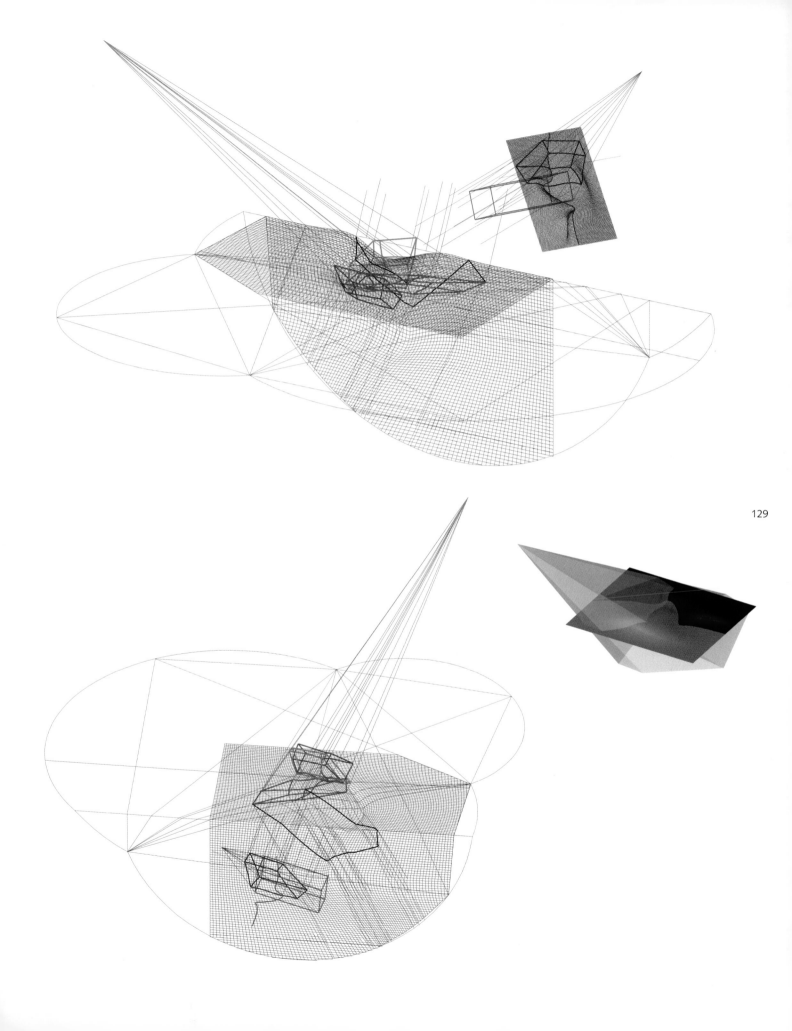

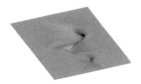

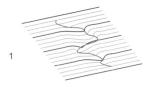

1

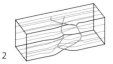

2

3

MONTAGUE HOUSE
(House on a Terminal Line)
1997–99

A terminal line deflects all but one of the orthogonal intersections of the surfaces that define the exterior envelope of the main body of this house. The absence of the line in an area otherwise continuous though ordinarily folded makes the whole surface appear taut.

A two-way structural skeleton is formed by laminated plywood members. The individual ribs are lapped, notched, spliced, interlocked, and bolted. The result is a system that provides support for various types of enclosures. Confined to gaps between structural members, glass panels are either fixed or operable windows. Wood-cement panels are shutters over screens, or walls backed up by condensed insulation.

A perspective projected from the main body is hollowed out to incorporate a carport with a garden on top. This compressed volume foregrounds the house from the roadside like a shield mirroring the house it protects. Rather than a conventional yard with a haphazard array of bushes, birdbaths, and flower beds, there is an open, gridded lawn. A mosaic of tiny floral, grass, and gravel plots, this surface is a variation on the porosity of the main house.

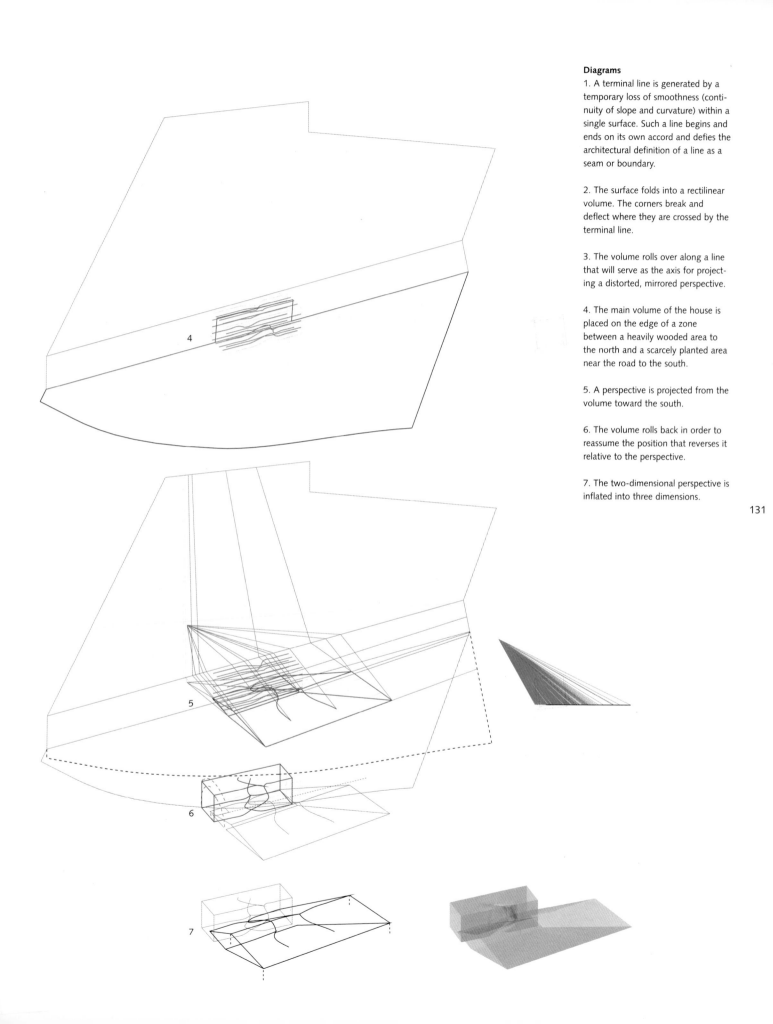

Diagrams

1. A terminal line is generated by a temporary loss of smoothness (continuity of slope and curvature) within a single surface. Such a line begins and ends on its own accord and defies the architectural definition of a line as a seam or boundary.

2. The surface folds into a rectilinear volume. The corners break and deflect where they are crossed by the terminal line.

3. The volume rolls over along a line that will serve as the axis for projecting a distorted, mirrored perspective.

4. The main volume of the house is placed on the edge of a zone between a heavily wooded area to the north and a scarcely planted area near the road to the south.

5. A perspective is projected from the volume toward the south.

6. The volume rolls back in order to reassume the position that reverses it relative to the perspective.

7. The two-dimensional perspective is inflated into three dimensions.

131

N

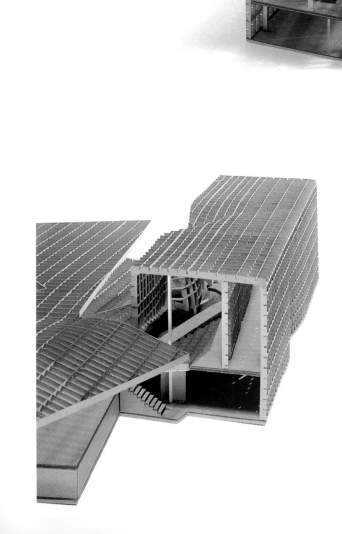

The plan consists of four adjoining areas: carport; entrance hall and studio/workshop apartment; living, dining, and kitchen spaces; and library and bedrooms. Two walls—the front boundary of the carport and the bookcase wall between library and bedrooms—run the length of the house and bracket an area that straddles all levels and programs. Breaking into the heart of this ensemble is a split switchback ramp. This circulatory device serves as an aperture between all four areas. No geometric system—orthogonal, curvilinear, or undulating—escapes it.

Because the space directly in front of the house is "behind and under" the front yard, it is audibly and visually protected from the road. Though frontal, this space is an informal car/terrace/skateboard court. Pedestrian ramp and driveway point the way into the house.

The living room level is relatively compressed in section while the library upstairs is rather lofty. In contraposition to the landscaped mosaic of the front yard, the structural membrane bordering the library produces a dramatically variegated wall of books that simultaneously performs as a façade to the four equal sized, though individually shaped, bedrooms behind. The library and adjacent terrace floors undulate according to the mapping of the "horizontal shadow volume" and in deference to southern light scoops that penetrate into the lower level.

The horizontally attenuated volume containing the carport extends along a downhill trajectory into the living room. As the ceiling over the carport slopes downward, the surface of the tarmac becomes a ramped floor to the upstairs library and terrace. Structural membrane and auxiliary columnar supports vie for perpendicular relationships to sloped and level ceilings and floors. A glass wall traverses and thermally divides the interior and exterior terrain like a fence in a subtly hilly landscape.

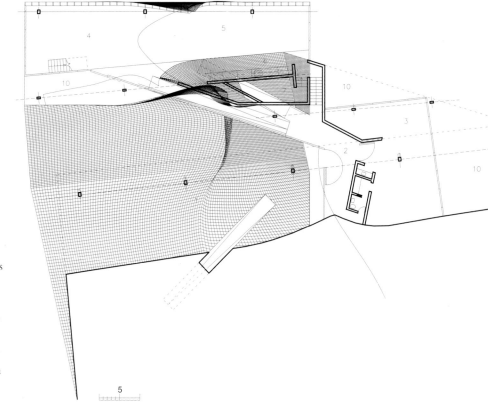

Program: A 3,800 square-foot house on a three-acre, wooded parcel in a low density residential area near Montague, New Jersey.

Materials: Laminated plywood structural beams milled by water jet will be clad in various materials including fiberglass, plywood, and sheet metal. Glass panels, screens, shelving, and other materials fill gaps in the framework.

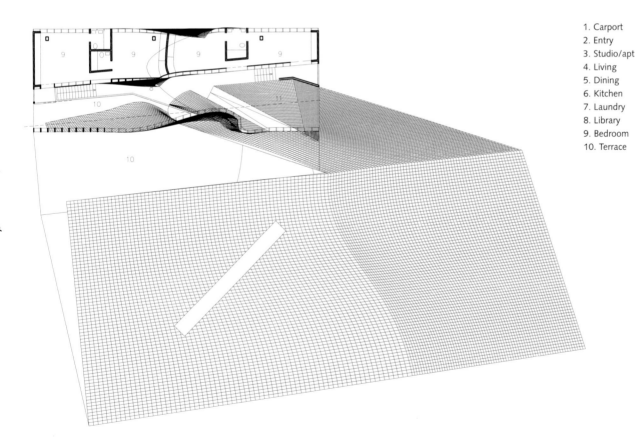

1. Carport
2. Entry
3. Studio/apt
4. Living
5. Dining
6. Kitchen
7. Laundry
8. Library
9. Bedroom
10. Terrace

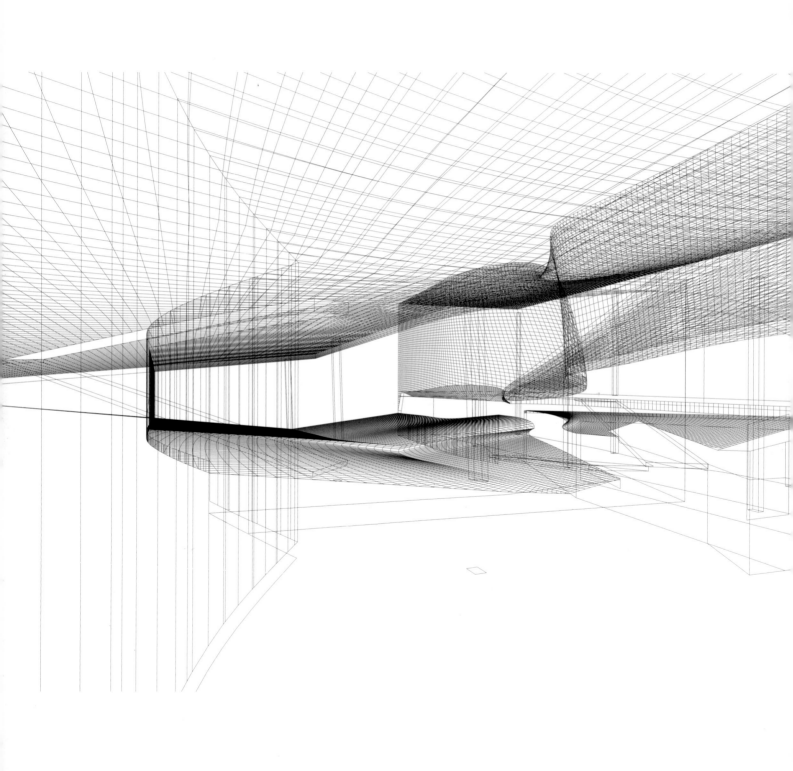

TORUS HOUSE
Columbia County, New York
1998–2000

In the Torus House, a curving line crosses the flat surfaces of the structure—walls, floors, and ceilings—causing them to undulate.[1] The straight lines between these otherwise conventional surfaces break and curve toward the curving line and thus appear to be folds in a single surface rather than orthogonal intersections between separate planes. This synthesis of normative features with a curvilinear element implicitly unifies a singular form alien to architecture—the torus—with several historically pervasive architectural types—the courtyard, the stairwell, the lightwell.[2]

Up to the point where the curving line dissolves into flatness, it divides a composite of surfaces as though they were a unified surface according to a larger scale of apportionment: top/bottom, left/right. The effect of this reapportionment—and the allusion to the torus—is to suspend familiar binaries: beginning/end, top/bottom, solid/void, inside/outside, open/closed. Antigravitational, multidirectional, and surrounded by space on all sides, a torus would ideally float unbound. Here, however, under the condition that it become a building, it can't. This insoluble prob-

lem causes the house to be elevated so that the outside spaces above and below appear as undifferentiated
as possible. In order to preserve the continuity of a
hollowed out state, as in a torus, compartmentalized
private rooms are appended to the periphery. From
below, the house appears somewhat urban as an aggre-
gate of contiguous blocks. But this arrangement is also
made to imply that one side of the membrane of the
torus has been thickened, stretched, and varied, so to
speak, in its vertical section in order to accommodate
different programs. This is made evident from the
roof, where the curving line and undulations blend
the individual volumetric components into an unbro-
ken surface that resembles features of the landscape
beyond.

Upon parking under the Torus House, one may
walk up the spiral staircase contained in the core,
bypass the interior of the house, arrive on the roof,
and survey the landscape. This sequence recalls the
voyeuristic pleasure of an invited guest who passes
through an empty house on his or her way to a back-
yard party. It also evokes the experience of an observa-
tion tower. Yet, in this case the vertical passageway is
relatively short and hovers above the ground. It is as if
a tower had been compressed, causing its top and bottom to splay into undulating horizontal surfaces. The

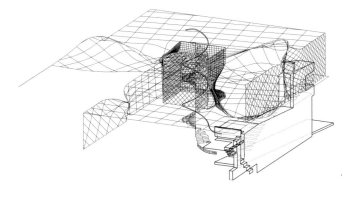

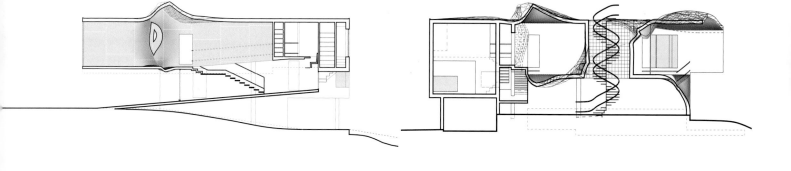

interior of the main body of the house can thus be
understood as the interval in a threshold between roof
and ground landscapes.

The actual threshold into the interior of the house
is a ramped foyer that passes between the living space
and the painter's workshop. The foyer ceiling is
formed by a ramp in the studio that terminates in a
landing that also serves as a kitchen table. There, a
bench allows one to sit at a table suspended over the
end of the foyer. This permits the simultaneous occu-
pation of kitchen, foyer, and studio, with a bifurcated
view of the living room (an easel painting studio) and
office, both on lower levels.

The client, painter Eric Wolf, will live in the com-
pact spaces adjacent to the two studios. The kitchen,
office, bedrooms, bathrooms, laundry/storage/mech-
anical rooms yield maximum square footage to the
two primary spaces and recall the ingenious space-
saving arrangements he devised for his Manhattan
apartment. In the Torus House, however, these tight
quarters are situated between the extensive wooded
site on one side and the commodious undivided interiors on the other.

Three bedrooms, each of different character,
accommodate different programmatic and seasonal
changes. The upper bedroom, the most private, has its

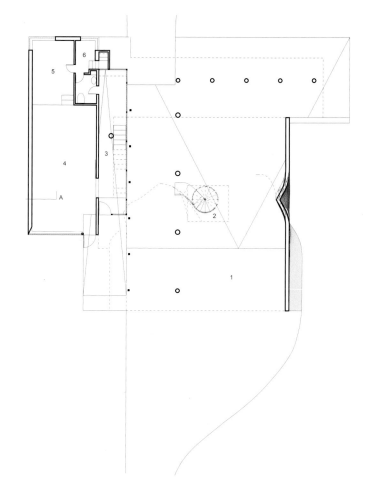

Program: A 3,104 square foot-house and studio for artist Eric Wolf in Columbia County, New York. The site is hilly. Woods alternate with open fields subdivided by rubble walls.

Primary materials: Poured-in-place concrete foundation. Steel columns support laminate wood structural ribs. Exterior cladding: sheet metal, lapped and attached with cleats, and soldered at seams and edges. Interior cladding: Strip plank hard wood in main room. Dry wall, plywood, and tile in other areas.

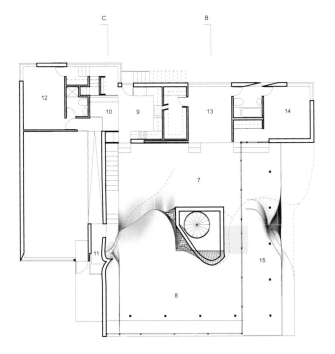

1. Carport
2. Stair to roof
3. Foyer
4. Workshop Studio
5. Painting storage
6. Laundry
7. Living
8. Easel painting stud
9. Kitchen
10. Kitchen table / upp
11. Office
12. Upper bedroom
13. Platform bedroom
14. Sleeping porch / b
15. Terrace

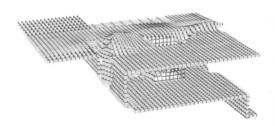

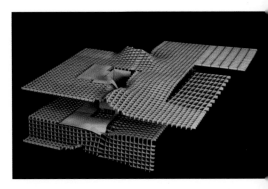

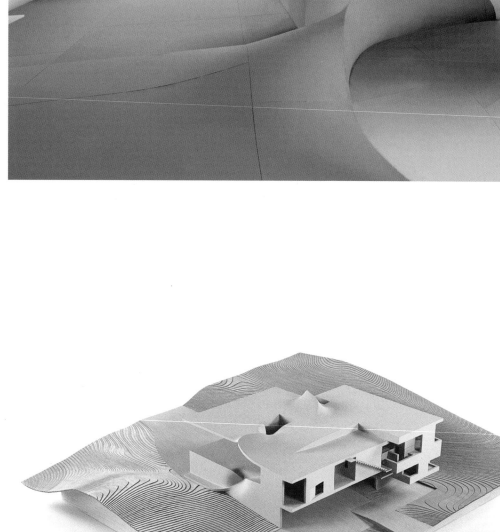

own bathroom and direct access to the studio work-shop, kitchen, and laundry. In conjunction with these rooms it comprises the portion of the house heated separately for year round use. During the warmer months, the easel painting studio doubles as a living room and in the winter may be used as a gallery. A bedroom extends from this space like a deeply recessed window seat. The floor of the bedroom becomes the platform for a bed placed directly next to the studio/living room. The third bedroom is like a sleeping porch that cantilevers beyond the outer edge of the living room terrace.

The house will be constructed in two phases, the first will correspond to the year round portion of the program. Concrete foundations and steel columns will support a two-way structural plywood laminate frame clad with strip planks, steamed and bent as in boat hull construction.

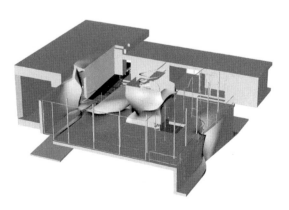

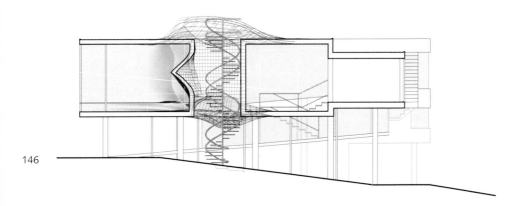

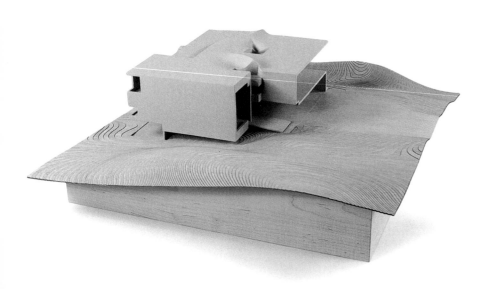

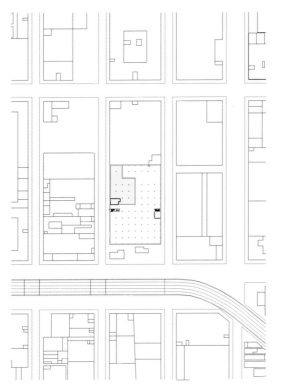

TEMPORARY MUSEUM OF MODERN ART

(Shortlist Proposal)
Long Island City, New York
2000

In the program for a temporary museum, architecture is called upon to be—as well as to stage—a singularly rare event. Its duration in such an instance depends upon its documentation. Architecture in this sense is analogous to a musical score, a notation within which resides a potential performance, rather than the melancholy and endurance of immanently anachronistic forms.

Such is the case with the 34,000 square foot exhibition space in Long Island City that will serve as a temporary Museum of Modern Art during the construction of an expansion to the museum's Manhattan complex. The Queens facility will be housed in the former Swingline Staple Company building, a 1970s blue brick, 141,000 square foot warehouse. The program for this project, created by Cooper Robertson & Partners of New York, called for the schematic design and development of a public entrance, lobby, ticketing, museum store, café, restrooms, and coat check. The areas allocated to the galleries will be designed by curators for specific exhibitions. No new exterior

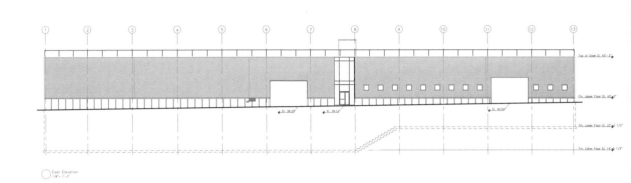

windows or skylights are to be added since, after the re-opening of MoMA in Manhattan, the warehouse will serve as a collection storage and process center.

The warehouse context of Long Island City is comparable to that of the SoHo and Chelsea neighborhoods of Manhattan, where artistic institutions preserve the facades and raw vitality of the pre-existing industrial fabric while interiors are designated as sites of transformation. Warehouses heighten the discovery of gallery spaces within, spaces that appear relatively conspicuous, refined, and distinctive only upon entry. In such contexts, expression is reserved for the interior. Embeddedness, and at times hiddenness, turn the experience of arrival into disclosure.

This proposal makes a comparable distinction between the existing boxy external shell and the exhibited space within. Rather than encapsulating the entire program behind a new provocative sign, façade or sculptural form, subtle alterations and enhancements to the exterior minimally indicate the presence of the museum. For example, a red banner intensifies the blue hue of the existing exterior. A redesigned window replacing the existing stair entry, though not part the museum space proper, indicates the inside, even if only deceptively. Finally, a deeply recessed gated portal (located in the current loading dock),

lends an intensified sense of tautness to the blue surface and draws one into the enigma of an otherwise impenetrable box. Such effects coincide with the notion of entry as event rather than museum as iconic image or object. If a three dimensional marker should ultimately be required, an installation atop the roof, such as Rachel Whiteread's *Water Tower* would supplant the need for a billboard.

In buildings such as the Swingline Warehouse, columnar grids have functioned primarily as technical apparatuses. Yet when understood aesthetically, the grid in modern architecture has represented an idealized universal space. Infinitely extendable yet impervious to change, structural grids release other elements —walls, primarily—from their obligation to support or regulate space. The grid has come to represent the essence of neutrality, flexibility, and, in the spatial paradigm of Mies, the dissolution of hierarchy between center and periphery so essential to modern art and architecture.

Mies's early houses exhibit columns that permit partitions to disperse and to dissolve boundaries between any potentially discrete spaces. In his later wide span pavilions, the evacuation of structural elements and their relegation to the periphery had the

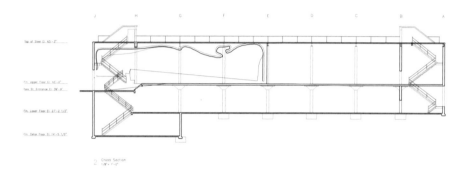

effect of centralizing space without recourse to classical elements such as domes or other hierarchical
forms. Yet, these great spaces were at once centripetal
and centrifugal. In Crown Hall (1956), and the New
National Gallery in Berlin (1962–68), a single cell of
space simultaneously announces centrality and propels
ones gaze out to the horizon.

Given that the Swingline warehouse does not
afford a view to the horizon, a street, or the attraction
of natural light, the temporary museum will need a
great lobby—an installation to behold in and of itself.
Yet the grid of columns, which Mies only used when
it was necessary to subdivide space, confounds the
desire for an undivided, coherent and yet dynamic
space of entry and gathering. In short, Swingline calls
for an inversion of the later Miesian model.

Movement was essential to both Mies's free
plans and empty pavilions. Within the confines of
immutable structural systems, movement became at
once an expressive force of form and the sponta-
neous, unchoreographed experience of the subject.
At Swingline, however, the inference of movement
is impeded by both the columns and the lack of
natural light.

Alternative paradigms of dynamic centralized
space such as Adolf Loos's houses and Frank Lloyd

Wright's Guggenheim, depend upon a dynamic
section with openings or circulation along the edges.
Equally important to such models is the delay of
entry, created through a spatial preamble.

But again, Swingline resists. It lacks sectional
variation (save for the depressed level of the existing
loading dock). Moreover, the location of the entire
lobby at the front edge of the building to the left,
rather than deep within it, though convincing in
terms of planning, is problematic according to these
dynamic spatial models. An entry sequence designed
to proceed in depth would leave most of the lobby
behind along with its opaque front wall to which
there would be little sequential incentive to return.
Alternatively, if the lobby is straightforwardly located
at the front wall of the building, the entrance becomes
unpostponed, too immediate.

The proposal thrives on the paradoxical nature of
MoMA's needs and its site constraints. It uses them to
deduce a process of transformation, merging structure
and spatial enclosure to create a sequence that seemingly relocates and centralizes the entire lobby.

The ceiling, as the least fettered domain, affords
the greatest opportunity for free play. Here it is possible to vary the section, imply coherence and create

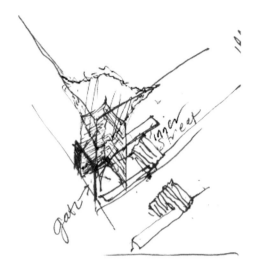

the illusion of spatial indeterminacy as well as the impression of hidden sources of natural light.

A certain column appears to stir up a dalliance with the ceiling. By exhibiting episodes of instability—curvilinear and oblique forms, geometrical "eddies"—the ceiling suggests that the columns are instruments of generative and dynamic forces.

The merger between the field of structural stability, the grid, and human movement on the one hand, and a geometrically dynamic surface responsive to light and unseen forces on the other, will take place along a line of convergence. The unrelenting flatness of the floor (with the exception of the sunken loading dock entry) and the columnar grid (with the exception of one missing row) will work to architectural advantage when contested by the freedom of the ceiling surface.

A wall originating from the edge of the ceiling hangs around the edge of the lobby like a drape. As the bottom edge rises obliquely from the entry (at which it is at its lowest point) toward the entrance to the galleries, space appears to recede behind the curtain wall before terminating in the actual wall of the galleries. Thus, the ceiling scatters programmatic elements to the periphery of the lobby, and fosters a multiplicity

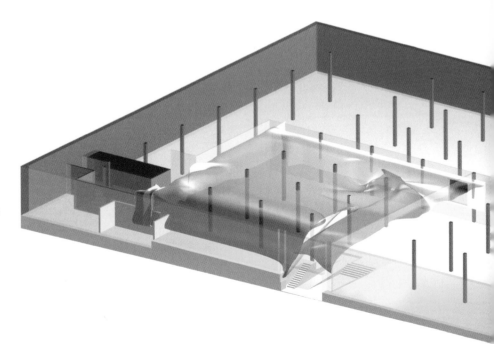

of criss-crossing itineraries and recessive, diagonal views. Such a pattern of program and movement implies that the lobby is embedded well within the building rather than on its edge.

The recessed portal creates an emphatic spatial corner. It has the effect of extending the space of the sidewalk perpendicularly into the shell of the building and establishing a diagonal trajectory. Entry proceeds from the recessed portal, either up a flight of stairs or a ramp to the left, both of which rise 3.5 feet within the confines of the existing loading dock. A window straight ahead, opposite the point of entry, offers a glimpse of the galleries beyond.

The Cafe and the bookstore are located along the front and left edges respectively. Ticketing and information desk are along the rear wall. The coat area and rest-rooms are situated in the far-left corner. The café rises slightly to form a distinct area overlooking the lobby. Entry to the gallery occurs behind the plane originating at the ceiling, through a door located in the corner of the lobby, diagonally across from the entry.

The location of the coatroom makes it necessary to traverse the lobby diagonally from the area near the window opposite the building entrance. Due to the origin of the ramp leading to the café, visitors leaving the galleries would cross diagonally back toward the front of the building.

Artificial light will be used as a compensatory element. Though natural light has always provided an orientation and connection to the world outside, at Swingline, incandescence and fluorescence will be used to choreograph varying degrees of luminosity and color value.

In temporary architecture, it is more appropriate for formal experimentation to take precedence than material luxury. Inexpensive materials—be they opaque or translucent—come to life under the pressure of form. Occasionally when form comes to rest and geometry is more straightforward, materials may become more refined.

153

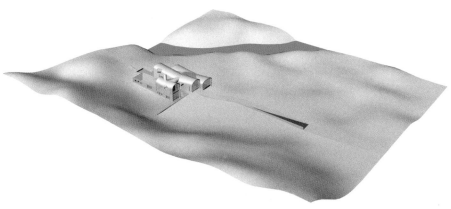

WU HOUSE

Burson, California

2000

In collaboration with Cameron Wu

In Wu House, geometric primitives—elliptical cylinders and cones—are positioned and intersected in such a way as to create sinuous lines that appear to be derived from topological surface geometry.

In the history of classical architecture, intersections of cylinders have almost exclusively followed two different types. The first, created by congruent perpendicular barrel vaults, produces a groin vault. The intersection line is an X in plan representing four individual surfaces contiguous along cusped borders **(a)**. A variant of this type is the case in which one of two crossing vaults extends no further than the apex, thereby creating a V, a single cusp **(b)**. The other type involves two vaults whose ridges are set at different levels and therefore are not tangent. This produces one or two curvilinear intersection lines **(c)**.

Usually either no lines or two lines are continuous with or connected to a single V cusp. In Wu House, however, a third surface passing through the point of tangency between the two previous tangent surfaces creates a Y intersection with a continuous trunk and a secondary branch. Because the first two surfaces are tangent at the point where the third intersects them, the new line of intersection between the first two combined and the third is continuous. Thus a continuous line divides the new surface from the previous two intersecting surfaces **(d)**. In Wu House, a fourth surface—a wall—is tangent with both one of the original two and the third. This causes the Y to close and to become a loop or lariat **(e)**.

a   b   c   d   e

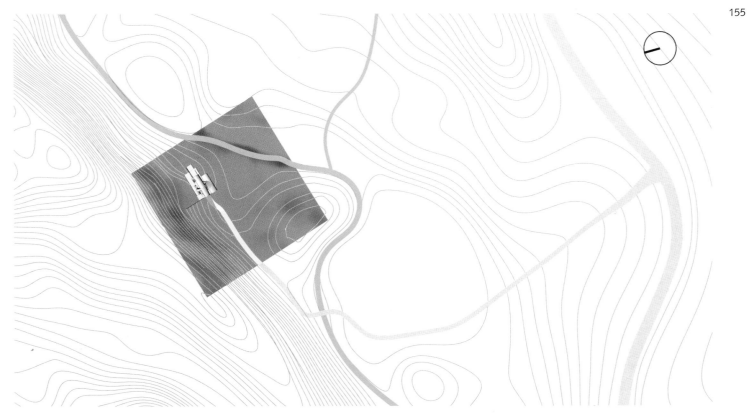

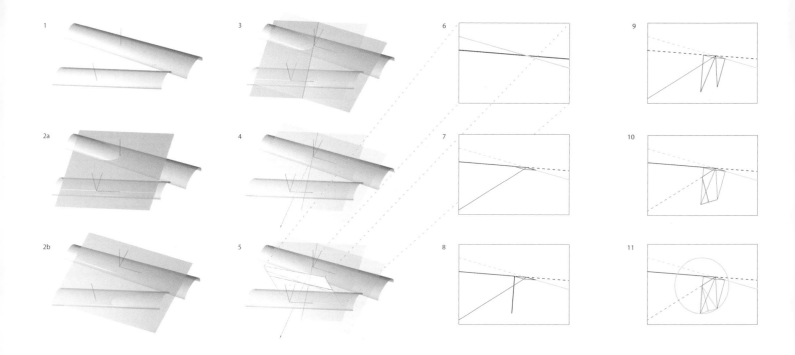

1   3   6   9

2a   4   7   10

2b   5   8   11

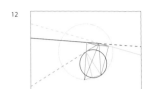

12

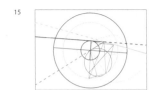

15

18

Construction of a cone tangent to two vaulted surfaces

1. Two vaulted surfaces with normals designated.

2. Planes tangent to each surface along straight line generators that contain endpoints of normals.

3. The intersection between tangent planes represents of the line of all possible apexes for the cone to be positioned.

4. Apex and central axis chosen.

5. Two-dimensional auxillary plane inserted perpendicular to cone axis.

6-16. Cross-section of the cone is determined by inscribing an ellipse of desired eccentricity between the traces (shown in yellow and blue) of the two planes of tangency on auxillary plane.

17. Auxillary plane re-inserted to three-dimensional construct.

18. Generators originating from apex sweep the path of the elliptical cross-section, producing the conic surface tangent to the vaults.

19. Two additional vaulted surfaces are introduced, each passing though the point of tangency between the cone and one of the original surfaces, resulting in the two saddles.

20. Cone is trimmed by the two lariats of intersection, resulting in the final configuration.

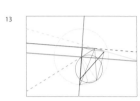

13

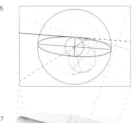

16

19

157

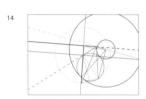

14

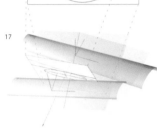

17

20

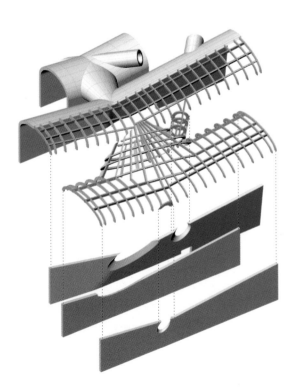

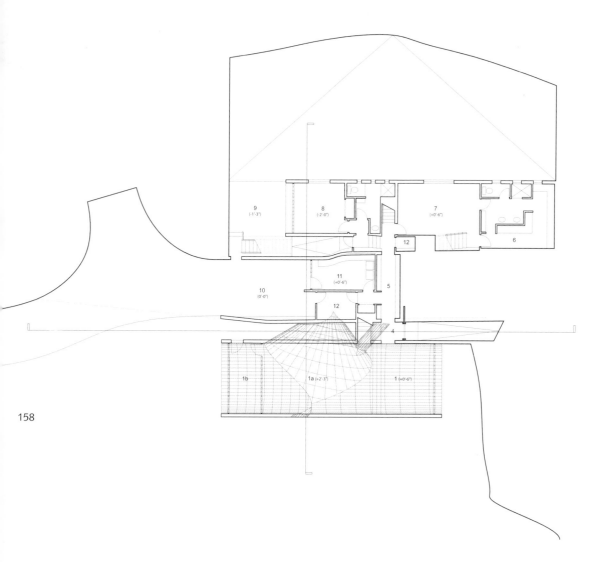

Program

A 2,600 square-foot house for a retired surgeon and his partner in the rolling arid foothills of the San Joaquin Valley of central California. The main massing of the house is composed three pairs of intersecting vaults, or "saddles." Cones pass between and intersect the saddles to produce joined lariats. These lines of intersection appear to be broken figure eights. At the outer limits of the two peripheral vaults, two lariats are the product of smaller elliptical cylinders that act as termini for the trio of saddles otherwise linked by cones. From the outer limits of the two peripheral saddles, the cylinders pierce back toward the central saddle as if to terminate the repetitive pattern of vaulted spaces.

The central saddle contains the focus of activity in the house: the kitchen and dining areas. It partially leans toward the neighboring living room saddle, allowing the conic connection between these two saddles to behave as an oculus from the kitchen. In the living room, the same cone appears as an extremely compressed domical figure and the oculus appears as if it were the ring of a distorted lantern.

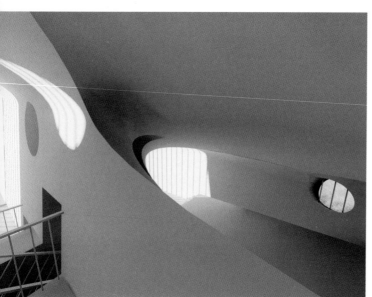

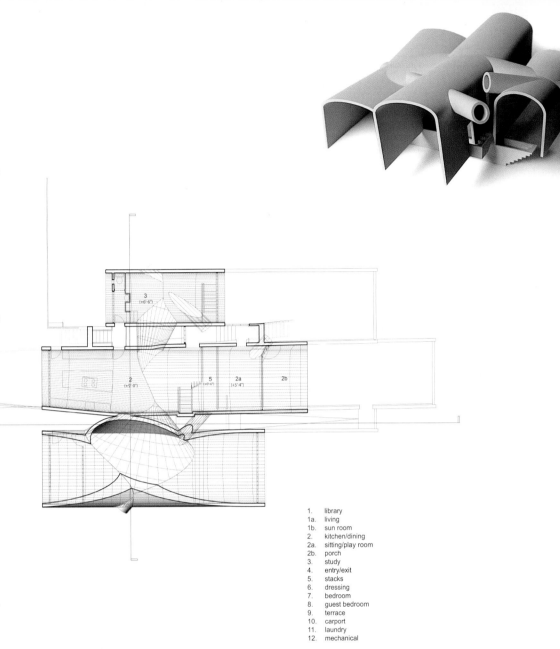

The third saddle, containing the study, is most evidently an independent entity. Its primary entry is from the courtyard, yet two passages link the study to the other two saddles. The first is a cone that joins it to the kitchen. It is too high for viewing and serves only for the passage of sound. The second passage is a corridor lined with books that, like a periscope, bypasses the kitchen and connects the study directly to the living room. The corridor cuts through and lies below the kitchen level. The central saddle appears divided by a moat that defines two separate occupyable areas that are spatially continuous with one another. The occupant is navigates the gap by circulating between the saddles. Passages act as counterparts to the conic and cylindrical passages for light, listening, and viewing.

159

Construction:
Poured in place concrete foundation. Masonry walls support laminate wood structural ribs milled by CNC water jet machine.

Exterior cladding: sheet terne metal, lapped, attached with cleats, and soldered at seams/edges.

Interior cladding: strip plank hard wood in main vaulted areas. Dry wall, plywood and tile in other areas.

1.   library
1a. living
1b. sun room
2.   kitchen/dining
2a. sitting/play room
2b. porch
3.   study
4.   entry/exit
5.   stacks
6.   dressing
7.   bedroom
8.   guest bedroom
9.   terrace
10. carport
11. laundry
12. mechanical

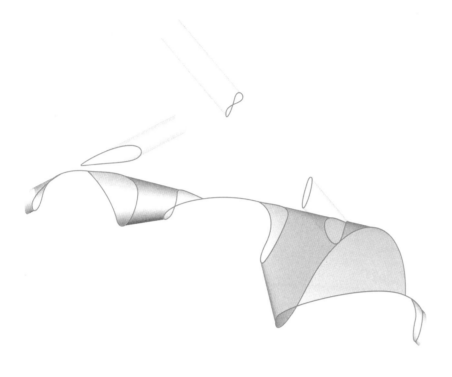

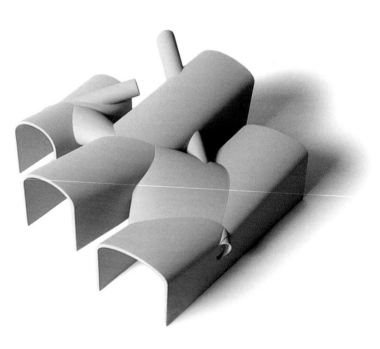

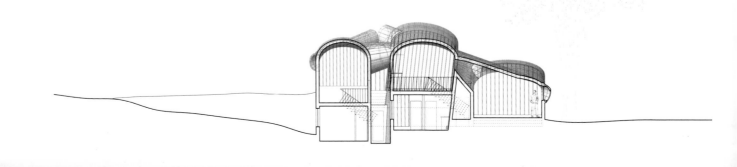

Preston Scott Cohen
Selected Bibliography

House in Austin, Texas
1982

166

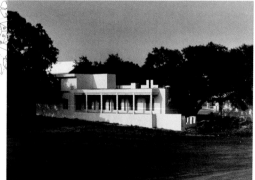

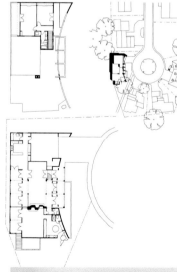

1985

Cohen, Preston Scott. "Project for Ca' Venier," in *Third International Exhibition of Architecture: Venice Project, Biennale Di Venezia*. Electra Editrice.

Investigations in Architecture: Eisenman Studios at the GSD: 1983–85. Boston: Harvard University Graduate School of Design.

1988

Cohen, [Preston] Scott. "House on Longboat Key," in *GSD Alumni: 1980–88*. New York: Steelcase Design.

1990

Cohen, Preston Scott. "Two Houses." *Assemblage* 13 (December): 72–87.

Somol, Robert. "No Place Like Home: Domesticating Assemblages." *Assemblage* 13 (December): 60–71.

1991

Sherer, Daniel. "The Politics of Formal Autonomy." *Assemblage* 15 (August): 99–103.

1993

Cohen, Preston Scott. "Cornered House," in *Harvard Architectural Review*, vol. 9. New York: Rizzoli.

Cohen, Preston Scott. "Allography." *GSD News* (winter/spring): 13.

"The Drawing Show." *Art New England* (fall).

1994

Cohen, Preston Scott. "Stereotomic Permutations." *Los Angeles Forum for Architecture* (December).

Cohen, Preston Scott. "Stereotomic Permutations." *ANY* (July): 61.

1995

Cohen, Preston Scott and Brooke Hodge, eds. *Eric Owen Moss: The Box*. New York: Princeton Architectural Press.

Chul, Kong. "A New Generation of Architects: Preston Scott Cohen, Greg Lynn." *Space Journal* (April): 30–7.

Early Childhood Facilities Fund (ECFF). *Patterns for Head Start Facilities*. Pennington, NJ: ECFF.

"Temples to Laughter and Reason." *World Architecture* (fall).

1996

The Architect as Seismograph: VI Venice Biennale International Exhibition of Architecture. Milan: Electra Editrice.

Cohen, Preston Scott. "Stereotomic Permutations," in *Architectural Design* (spring): 89–92.

Cohen, Preston Scott. "Stereotomic Permutations." *Appendix* 3 (spring): 46–73.

Weinstock, Michael. "Scott Cohen's Projections." *AA Files* (June): 94–6.

1998

Cohen, Preston Scott. "The Anamorphic Imperative." *RISD Works* 2 (fall).

"Progressive Architecture Awards." *Architecture* (April): 74–7. (Award for House on a Terminal Line.)

1999

Codrington, Andrea. "Home Peep Show." *Metropolitan Home*, July/August 1999, 167–9.

Cohen, Preston Scott. "Torus House," *Arch +* (October): 20–1.

Denbury, Jo. "Predictomania." *Elle Decoration* (London), July.

Giovannini, Joseph. "House Rules." *Elle Décor*, June/July.

Hays, K. Michael. "Torus House at Old Chatham, New York." *Domus* (December): 30–3.

Hubertus, Adam. "The Un-Private House," *Arch +* (October): 20–1.

Iovine, Julie. "The Last Gasp for the American Living Room." *New York Times*, 28 January.

Kuhnert, Nikolaus and Angelika Schnell, "Blobs and Boxes," *Arch +* (October): 20–1.

Riley, Terence. *The Un-Private House*. New York: Museum of Modern Art.

Smith, Roberta. "Drop-Dead Beauty and Luxe, With an Intimate Index of Change," *New York Times*, 2 July.

Sudjic, Deyan, with Tulga Beyerle. *Home: The Twentieth-*

Century House. London: Calmann & King.

Withers, Jane. "The Future of Home," *Harper's Bazaar*, June.

2000

"Ausgehohlt: Unkonvenionelle Strukturen im Torus-Haus," *DBZ–Deutsche Bauzeitschrift* (June): 32–3.

Beke, Laszlo, Adele Eisenstein, and Miklos Peternak. *Perspektiva*. Budapest: Mucsarnok/Kunsthalle.

Cohen, Preston Scott. "Regular Anomalies: The Case of the Tubular Embrasure at the Sacristy of San Carlo ai Catinari in Rome," in *AA Files* (summer): 46–56.

Cohen, Preston Scott and Robert Levit, "Bona Fide Modernity," in *Assemblage* 41.

Cohen, Preston Scott. "Terminal Lines," *Architecture and Urbanism* (February): 90–105.

Cohen, Preston Scott. "Torus House," in *Global Architecture: GA Houses Project 2000*. Tokyo: A.D.A. Edita.

"47th Annual Progressive Architecture Awards," *Architecture*, April.

Hays, K. Michael. "Terminal Desire: A Note on Scott Cohen's Recent Projects," *Architecture and Urbanism (A&U)*, (February): 106–9.

Muschamp, Herbert. "The Modern is Considering a Temporary Site in Queens." *New York Times*, 26 January.

Muschamp, Herbert. "Modern Chooses Architect." *New York Times*, 10 February.

Pollak, Sabine. "The End of the Familar Home?" *Architecktur Fachmagazine* (March): 6–8.

Riley, Terence. "Preston Scott Cohen" in *10x10*. London: Phaidon.

Safran, Yehuda. "Guide for the Perplexed," *Lotus* 104, 70–5.

Sherer, Daniel. "A Disquieting Conversation; Manfredo Tafuri and Operative Criticism," in Guido Canella, ed., *La Critica Operativa Atti del Convegno Internazionale* Promosso dal Departimento di Progettazione Architettonica Politechnico di Milano. Milan.

Weinzierl, Ulrich. "Drawing the Curtain," *Frankfurter Allgemeine Zeitung, 24* February.

2001

"Preston Scott Cohen," *Visionaire 35*.

Exhibitions

1985

Third International Exhibition of Architecture: Venice Project, Biennale Di Venezia, (group exhibition).

1986

Investigations in Architecture: Eisenman Studios at the GSD: 1983–85, Harvard Graduate School of Design (GSD) main gallery, (group exhibition.)

1987

RISD Alumni Exhibition, Rhode Island School of Design, Department of Architecture (group exhibition.)

1988

GSD Alumni, 1980–1988, Steelcase Design Gallery, New York; GSD gallery, (group exhibition).

1989

Recent Work: Faculty of the Department of Architecture, Wexner Center for the Arts, University Gallery for Fine Art, Ohio State University, (group exhibition).

1990

House on Siesta Key, GSD currents gallery, (solo exhibition).

1992

On Hold: Young Architects Awards, Architectural League of New York, (group exhibition).

1993

The Drawing Show, Boston Center for the Arts, (group exhibition).

1994

Stereotomic Permutations, GSD currents gallery, (solo exhibition).

1996

The Architect as Seismograph, VI Venice Biennale International Exhibition of Architecture, (group exhibition).

An Addition of Perspectives, GSD currents gallery, (solo exhibition).

Preston Scott Cohen: Recent Projects, Architectural Association of London, (solo exhibition).

1997

Tafuri's Ricerca/Drawing as Research, GSD gallery, (group exhibition).

1998

1998 Progressive Architecture Awards, Rensselaer Polytechnic Institute, (group exhibition).

24 Hrs: Drawings, Gallery Joe, Philadelphia, PA, (group exhibition).

1999

The Un-Private House, Museum of Modern Art, New York; MAK, Vienna; Walker Art Center, Minneapolis; Armand Hammer Museum of Art, UCLA, Los Angeles, (group exhibition).

Home, Glasgow 1999 International Exhibition of Architecture, (group exhibition).

Perspektiva, Mucsarnok/Kunsthalle, Budapest, (group exhibition).

Drawing the Line, Philadelphia Art Alliance, (group exhibition).

2000

Regular Anomalies, Columbia University School of Architecture, Planning and Preservation, New York, (solo exhibition).

2001

Folds, Blobs, and Boxes, Heinz Architectural Center, Carnegie Museum of Art, Pittsburgh, Joseph Rosa, Curator, (group exhibition).

Project Credits

Contested Symmetries: Palazzo Gambara
Assistants: Tina DiCarlo (research), Kay Vorderwuelbecke (background rendering)

Regular Anomalies: Villa Tauro
Research assistant: Tina DiCarlo

Elliptical Congruencies: The Tubular Embrasure
Project collaborators: Cameron Wu, Tina DiCarlo (research)

Inversive Projections: Taylorian Perspective Apparatus
Project collaborator: Cameron Wu

House in Austin, Texas, 1982 (p. 168)
Client: Harris and Carol Cohen

House on Longboat Key
Client: Harris and Carol Cohen
Consulting architect: Dan Ionescu, Sarasota, FL

House on Siesta Key
Client: David Bitterman

Wydra House Addition
Client: Nancy Lee Wydra

Cornered House
Client: Charles Ray
Young Architects Award, Architectural League of New York, 1992

Muss Corridor
Client: Joan and Jeffrey Muss
Drawing assistant: John Schneider

Stereotomic Permutations
House WCIAU:
Assistants: Simon Hsu (Computer modeling), Wade Stevens (model)

Presso Villa Marco III:
Assistants: Chris Hoxie (Computer modeling), Brian Bell (model)
Graphics: Mark Careaga

Stilicho Duplex
Model: David Yocum
Duplex Project assistant: Sam Lasky
Site Model: Josh Heitler
Photoshop montage: John Malone

Honorable Mention: Temple to Laughter and Reason Competition, 1994

Patterns for Head Start Facilities
Competition, mention
Project team: Brian Bell, David Yocum

Addition to the Prado Museum Competition
Computer modeling, rendering: Chris Hoxie
Competition presentation team: Jay Berman, Larry Burks, Josh Heitler, Andrea Lamberti, Matt LaRue, Wade Stevens, Abby Turin
Biennale presentation team: S. Kirsten Gay, Mark Careaga, Ana Sotrel
Model: Zeke Brown

Montague House
Client: Richard Boscarino
Project collaborator: Chris Hoxie
Presentation assistants: Alexandra Barker, Michael Samra
1998 Progressive Architecture Award

Torus House
Client: Eric Wolf
Project team: Alexandra Barker, Chris Hoxie, Eric Olsen
Model: Darell Fields, Scott Cohen, Aaron D'Innocenzo, Judy Hodge
2000 Progressive Architecture Award

Temporary MoMA
Shortlist proposal for the Museum of Modern Art, Glenn Lowry, Director
Project collaborator: Cameron Wu
Presentation Assistants: Angus Eade, Steven Lee

Wu House
In collaboration with Cameron Wu
Client: Dr. Yenching Wu
Renderings: Chris Hoxie

Illustration Credits

Contested Symmetries

figs. 1.1, 1.3, 1.13, 1.15
Carlo Perogalli, Maria Grazia Sandri, Vanni Zanella, *Ville Della Provincia di Brescia, Lombardia 3* (Rusconi Libri S.p.A., Edizioni SISAR, Milano, 1985). Reprinted by permission of Roberto Nardini, GPP Industrie Grafiche.

fig. 1.4
Carlo Perogalli, Maria Grazia Sandri, *Ville Delle Province di Cremona e Mantova, Lombardia 5* (Edizioni SISAR Milano, 1973), 296. Reprinted by permission of Roberto Nardini, GPP Industrie Grafiche.

fig. 1.5
Santino Lange, *Ville Delle Province di Como, Sandrio, e Varese, Lombardia 2* (Edizioni SISAR Milano, 1968),138. Reprinted by permission of Roberto Nardini, GPP Industrie Grafiche.

figs. 1.6, 1.7, 1.9
Carlo Perogalli, Maria Grazia Sandri, *Ville Della Provincia di Bergamo e Brescia, Lombardia 3* (Edizioni SISAR Milano, 1969). Reprinted by permission of Roberto Nardini, GPP Industrie Grafiche.

figs. 1.8, 1.14
Adriano Alpago Novello, *Ville Della Provincia di Belluno, Veneto 1* (Edizioni SISAR Milano, 1968). Reprinted by permission of Roberto Nardini, GPP Industrie Grafiche.

fig. 1.10
Photo:Antelmi Misericordia in Elena Bassi, *Palazzi di Venezia*, Stamperia di Venezia Editrice, Venezia 1976),104, ill. 97-98

fig. 1.11
Jim Ackerman, *Distance Points* (MIT Press,1991) 313, ill. 10.8. Photograph courtesy of author; plan from Chiolini, *I caratteri distributivi degli antichi edifici*

fig. 1.12
Richard J. Goy, *Venetian Vernacular Architecture: Traditional Housing in the Venetian Lagoon*, (Cambridge Univ. Press 1989), 134-135, ill. 83. Reprinted by permission of author.

Chapter 2: Regular Anomalies

figs. 2.1-2.4, 2.6-2.8
Adriano Alpago Novello, *Ville Della Provincia di Belluno, Veneto 1* (Edizioni SISAR Milano, 1968). Reprinted by per-

mission of Roberto Nardini, GPP Industrie Grafiche.

fig. 2.9
Elena Bassi, *Palazzi di Venezia*, Stamperia di Venezia Editrice, Venezia 1976), 87, ill.72

Chapter 3: Elliptical Congruencies

fig. 3.7
Athanasius Kircher, *Musurgia Universalis* (Rome: ex typographia hearedum, Franscisci Corbelletti, 1650)

fig. 3.8
Dr. Jiri Zahradnik, Dr. Jiri Cihar, *Animal World*, 1963

fig. 3.9
Pablo Picasso, "Dora Maar Seated", © 2000 Estate of Pablo Picasso / Artist Rights Society (ARS), New York. Photograph reproduced with permission of Art Resource, New York

Stilicho Duplex

Model photographs: Tom Stankowicz

Patterns for Head Start Facilities

Model Photographs: Tom Stankowicz

Competition for the Expansion and Re-planning of the Museo del Prado, Madrid

Juan Antonio Gaya Nuno, *Historia del Museo del Prado (1819-1969)*, (Editorial Everest 1969), 116, ill. 124, 125; 208, ill. 230

Albert F. Calvert, *Madrid*, (The Spanish Series,1906), plate 15

Model photographs: Pavlina Lucas

Montague House

Model photographs Anton Grassl

Torus House

Model photographs: Doug Cogger

Temporary MoMA

Site photograph/montage: Steven Lee

Wu House

Model photographs: Doug Cogger

Acknowledgments

This book has benefited from the contributions of many friends and colleagues. First, I thank Miles Ritter for introducing me to projective geometry and, in particular, Taylorian perspective. I am also privileged to have been tutored by Robin Evans. The pedagogy of Peter Eisenman has provided a compelling example for all who consider architecture to be a disciplined experiment. K. Michael Hays's work on autonomy is decisive to the continuing reception of this experiment.

The ideas in this book have been galvanized by many conversations over the years. I would like to thank Robert Gutman, Toshiko Mori, Eric Owen Moss, Peter Rose, Dan Schodek, and Edward Sekler for responding to questions about ramifications of geometry for practice and construction; Alan Colquhoun, Rodolphe el-Khoury, Jeffrey Kipnis, Detlef Mertins, and Hashim Sarkis for discussing the theoretical importance of complexity in architecture; Luis Rojo for compelling critiques of countless buildings and projects; and interlocutor Robert Levit for incisive accounts of predicaments past and present.

I am indebted to Dan Sherer for numerous insights and references regarding norms and exceptions; Mirka Benes for her detailed translations and bibliographical advice on wonder and curiosity; and James Ackerman for discussing his seminal work on villas and renaissance perspective.

A number of friends and colleagues contributed valuable advice and support during the making of the projects in this book, including Tim Costello, Sue Evans, Homa Fardjadi, Kenneth Frampton, Kevin Kieran, Ralph Lerner, Jonathan Levi, Rodolfo Machado, John Malone, Ted Marks, Gerry Mryglot, Linda Pollak, Monica Ponce de Leon, Ed Robbins, Paul Robertson, Stanley Saitowitz, Brigitte Shim, Nigel Smith, Ivan Stillerman, Nader Tehrani, Sarah Whiting, and Kelly Wilson. Brooke Hodge has consistently brought my work to the attention of others including Terence Riley, whose support has been invaluable. The Torus House would not have been possible without Eric Wolf's distinctive program and his many critical interventions.

I would like to thank the publishers and editors of the journals and anthologies in which many of the projects in this book have previously appeared. Among them, Mohsen Mostafavi, Pamela Johnston, and Mark Rappolt at the Architecture Association in London deserve special mention for their editorial work on terminal lines and the tubular embrasure. For the publication of this book, I owe many thanks to Clare Jacobson, Kevin Lippert, Mark Lamster, and Deb Wood of Princeton Architectural Press.

I have Harvard to thank for funding much of the research and production that went into the analytic projects of the book. Peter Rowe and Pat Roberts have repeatedly been generous with both personal and institutional support, resources and advice. Many of my students have been especially supportive and indulgent. I have benefited immensely from the knowledge and resourcefulness of Lucia Alias, Josh Comaroff, and Mike Price, and from the research assistance and editorial acumen of David Goodman, Jeannie Kim, Abby Turin, Becky Vas, and especially Tina di Carlo, who made invaluable contributions to the chapters on the villas and the sacristy and persevered in spite of my many insufferable about-faces and digressions.

Gratitude is especially due to those who contributed to the making of the projects. Cameron Wu's work on the Tubular Embrasure and the Taylorian Apparatus was indispensable to the exacting realization of these investigations. Chris Hoxie's contributions to the later projects are immeasurable; his acute eye and countless hours of deft experimentation with form and software put me greatly in his debt.

Rafael Moneo, with his indefatigable inquisitiveness and penetrating doubt, has been a constant source of inspiration. Mack Scogin, mentor, critic, and confidant, created a climate conducive to fruitful experimentation. I am thankful to Jorge Silvetti for opening my eyes to architectural pleasures previously subject to censure and for having fostered an audience receptive to these forms of investigation.

Finally, I would like to thank Jane Nelson, Harris Cohen, Shelley Fudge, Rick Cohen, and Carol Cohen for their tireless care and encouragement.

In all of our travels, Line Aldebert has, more than she can know, enriched and sustained my work throughout.

About the Author

Preston Scott Cohen was born in Asheville, North Carolina in 1961. He holds BFA and B.Arch degrees from the Rhode Island School of Design and an M.Arch from the Harvard University Graduate School of Design, where he now serves on the faculty as an Associate Professor of Architecture. He has received numerous awards for his work, including Progressive Architecture Awards in 1998 and 2000. He was also a winner of the Architectural League of New York's Young Architects Competition in 1992.